# A Blending of Bittersweet
# Memories

*Best wishes,*

Best Wishes!

# A Blending of Bittersweet Memories

## Emily Israel Hoffman

### with Molly Each

P.O. Box 10936
Chicago, IL 60610
www.bittersweet-memories.com
emily@bittersweet-memories.com
Twitter: @bittersweet-memories
Blog: ablendingofbittersweetmemories.blogspot.com
Facebook:http://www.facebook.com/pages/Chicago-
IL/wwwbittersweet-memoriescom/173665582248?ref=ts

"I don't know what it is about food your mother makes for you, especially when it's something anyone can make—pancakes, meat loaf, tuna salad—but it carries a certain taste of memory."
—Mitch Albom, *One More Day*

*Photo of Renée and Emily -- 11 months before Renée passed away.*
*Photographed by Carrie Ratliff on February 17, 2005.*

*This book is dedicated to the memory of my mother, Renée Israel, the strongest, most amazing woman I've ever met. While I still struggle with the fact that I only had 22 years with her, I'm grateful for every single moment she was in my life—and for all of the memories she left behind.*

*And to all those who have lost someone near and dear to them: hold them close, always.*

# Table of Contents

# Emily's Story

My mother's prized possession was her dining room table. Fifty feet long and crafted from dark wood, it seated thirty people comfortably (forty if we squished together), and stretched the entire length of our dining room. Every Sunday night when I was growing up, this dining room table was the culinary hotspot of our suburban Chicago community, as friends, family, and colleagues gathered to indulge in my mother's home-cooked meals. My mom, Renée Israel, felt most at home in the kitchen, and playing host to a crew of hungry friends and family—whether it was a holiday, a charity event or just an average Tuesday night with her husband and three daughters—was what she did best. Still, it was Sunday dinner where she truly thrived. From creating a festive tabletop to writing out playful place cards or designing an elaborate menu and grocery shopping, she reveled in the entire dinner-party process. It was how she showed her love for her family, her friends, and my dad, David.

As a kid, I loved to watch her cook. I would bring my homework into the kitchen and work on my multiplication tables while she effortlessly chopped vegetables, beat eggs, and scribbled little notes on scratch paper. Occasionally, she'd ask for my help with a small task— opening the cottage cheese container, for example—and I nearly burst with excitement at the opportunity to contribute to the dinner. As I got older, my Sunday dinner responsibilities increased. Instead of mere spectator occasionally called upon to help, I became my mom's sous chef. I helped create the menu, do the shopping, put the table together, chop the vegetables, and assemble the dishes, all under the watchful eye of my expert mother. At an early age, I learned to love the warm feeling of making something and learned to delight in the joy of feeding friends and family. I owe my wealth of knowledge about cooking and hospitality entirely to my mom and her Sunday night dinners.

In addition to her roles as effortless hostess and delightful cook, Renée Israel was many other things: a loving mother, a devoted wife, a friend to everyone she met, a breast cancer survivor, and a joy to be around, thanks in part to her infectious laugh and her ability to make anyone smile. In short, she was my best friend and my hero.

In 2001, as I was working through my freshman year at Lake Forest College, my mom began to have trouble climbing the stairs, and she couldn't seem to shake a horrible cough. After dozens of tests, our fears were confirmed. The breast cancer that had been in remission for twenty years was back, now in Stage four Worse still, some of the cells had moved into her lungs, so her disease was coupled with equally advanced lung cancer. The doctors gave her two years.

They didn't know Renée Israel. For the next four years, my mother fought like a heavyweight champ to stay alive. I moved home to care for her. Since I was the one who knew her day-to-day life best, I became her right hand. I slept in the hospital when she stayed overnight and drove her to complete her errands. As the disease progressed, I bathed her, dressed her, and helped blow-dry her hair before she lost it. Suddenly, our roles had flipped. Now, I was taking care of my mother rather than being cared for by her. Sometimes, she'd even call me "moms."

As her condition worsened, she was forced to step out of the kitchen and I was forced to step in. Sunday dinners continued, but now I was at the helm, churning out her staple dishes: spinach pie, green bean casserole, orzo, kugel. While I stirred up fruit compote and whipped out mashed potatoes, my mom sat in her bed, constructing menus, dictating the appropriate cooking equipment and tabletop décor and answering my questions over an intercom. Even in the last few months, when she couldn't get out of bed to join us, we still held Sunday dinners religiously, following my mom's careful instructions to a T. Simply knowing that our home was filled with joy and love filled her with a sense of peace

In January 2006, my mother lost her battle with breast and lung cancer.

While my friends graduated from college, pursued their dream jobs, moved across the country and lived it up, I stood stuck like a deer in the headlights, unsure of where to go and what to do, unable to pull myself out of bed or put myself together. I ignored phone calls from family and friends, getting myself out of my bed just long enough to make sure my equally grief-stricken dad had dinner each night. The five stages of grief—denial, anger, bargaining, depression, acceptance—spun over and over again a mess of out-of-control emotions. Finally, after eleven months, I woke up and realized I couldn't live with myself anymore. I checked myself into grief rehabilitation in Pacific Palisades, California. I needed to learn how to live again.

Up at eight a.m. each day, my days were heavily scheduled with exercise, private therapy sessions, group therapy sessions, nutrition classes, yoga, and fun activities. Unable to stay in bed all day, I relearned how to function like a normal person. I felt energetic again. In just one month at the grief center, I did more than I had in an entire year.

Upon returning to Chicago, I started working at a commercial real estate development firm, but nothing felt fulfilling. I had no passion for it and quickly lost the sense of purpose I had gained at the grief center. Phases spun quickly through me. One day I would be angry that she was gone, and the next day I felt bound to my bed with depression. I never felt like I was put back together; to some extent, I still don't. One night, unable to shake a craving for Ma's kugel, I pulled out her recipe and started to cook.

Once I began, I felt a wave of calm wash over me. The sound of eggs whisking in a bowl, the smell of cinnamon, the feel of the dough in my hands—they all brought to mind vivid images and memories of my mother. I instantly felt as though she was at my side, cooking kugel with me. After a few meals, I realized that I craved that feeling of closeness with my mom, and I found myself in the kitchen more and more, churning out classic mom dishes like Monday night spaghetti and her orzo salad.

As I was the one who had been by her side in the kitchen while growing up, hosting family dinners and holiday gatherings naturally fell onto my plate. The role of the chef and hostess was once my mother's, then it became ours together, and now it is mine alone. On the first Rosh Hashanah after I came home from California, I made dinner for my family. When the kugel came out, it was as though my mother was with us. Carrying on her recipes and her traditions became an act of carrying on her legacy. For my entire family, she was present at that meal, as she has been at every family meal since.

The constant journey of learning how to deal with my grief has been at times heart wrenching. At other times, enlightening. Many people told me to research Elizabeth Kubler-Ross's classic five stages of grief, but I found her phases (denial, anger, bargaining, depression, acceptance) too black and white to describe the constant flux—the way that I could be happy and smiling one moment and then suddenly overcome by a wave of sadness the next. With this book, I sought to capture a different process of grieving. Its chapters are divided and named to more accurately describe *my* journey: what I needed to find and where I found it; how I grew; and what helped me along. When I simply needed to survive, I immersed myself in ritual. When I needed to feel a true connection to my friends and family, I began to nurture myself and others. When I needed to heal through a momentary burst of joy, I found those who could make me laugh the hardest. Eventually, connecting with my creative side allowed me to look back at my whole experience with gratitude. It's my hope that I have captured grief as a constant journey, one with highs and lows that, no matter how much time has passed, can take you in any direction at any given moment.

For me, sharing stories has been essential in dealing with the loss of my mother. Nothing makes me feel more connected than chatting with someone who knows exactly what I'm going through. At the same time, it has been inspiring and eye-opening to hear stories from others who come from a completely different place. It would have been easy to write a cookbook that simply featured my mother's recipes, but truthfully, the stories interest me just as much as the food. Our world is so chaotic, and I love the way that even a short anecdote forces you to stop, look outside yourself, and think about the world in a new way. Death is a topic that many people don't want to discuss, but given that it's one of life's certainties, it seems wise to channel our grief into something positive. That's where *A Blending of Bittersweet Memories* comes in. Whipping together delectable recipes with heartwarming memories, this book is as much a light-hearted guide through grief as it is a cookbook for any occasion. In honor of my mother, I encourage you to mix up a recipe with your loved ones, gather around the table, and spend some time savoring food and stories.

# Chapter 1

## Survival through Ritual

**"All sorrows are less with bread." —Miguel Cervantes, *Don Quixote***

What's the strangest part about grief? The way it can hit you out of nowhere, like a sack of flour, weakening your body, pummeling your spirit and making you want to crawl back into bed for weeks. Even five years later, now that I've accepted and adjusted to my mother's loss, a wave of grief can still whack me from out of the blue. I feel like I've lost her all over again, the pain as raw and fresh as it was in the first few weeks after her death.

When these waves of grief wash over me, I find my way to the kitchen. I take out my mother's favorite recipes and lose myself in the ritual of cooking. With one part of my mind fully focused on the chopping-mincing-mixing-slicing-dicing, the other part can wander, letting the sights, sounds, smells, and motions conjure up memories of my mom. As I measure heaping tablespoons and grease pans, I find myself mimicking her kitchen habits: cooking in tapered sweatpants, using her favorite oversized yellow mixing bowl, pulling out a pad of paper to create my own cooking and table-setting prep list. It's through this ritual, used during an intense haze of sadness, that I realize I will survive the waves of grief. I will tread through.

Everyone has coping rituals: survivors might pray or attend church, write letters to their lost loved one, or visit a place that their loved one enjoyed. They may talk to that person—either out loud or in their mind. But it seems that no matter what, food is always an essential tool for coping. We emulate and honor our lost loved ones by making the dishes they loved. Since my mother's death, food rituals have been essential to my family's survival—just the way my mom would have wanted. We gather on her favorite holidays and special occasions to prepare kugel or grandma's chicken, even shopping for the ingredients at the same places my mother did. We honor her by carrying on the traditions she established. We joke, we laugh, we talk about what's happening in our lives, and we reconnect in a way that my mother would have loved. As I savor the taste of familiar cuisine and the sight of my family, her memory glows brightly. I'm nourished as much by the food as I am by my family's presence and my mother's memory.

These rituals do even more than soothe my grief-stricken soul; they keep my mother's legacy alive. My sisters and I do our best to recreate the feeling of warmth that my mother created, savoring it again and again and again, hoping that our children can feel the same sensations. We emulate her holiday process down to the smallest detail—starting our menu lists days in advance, creating an elaborate tabletop, cooking with a spring in our step—eager to pass on even a little bit of the excitement and anticipation that we felt. We prep and feed our families the same foods, hoping that they too, feel the love and nourishment that we felt. And built into each ritual are stories about my mother, which we tell and retell with smiles on our faces and tears in our eyes, ensuring that her memory never, ever fades.

When grief attempts to pull me down, ritual is a lifeboat to carry me back to the present moment. I feel alive, and I am reminded that even in the most painful, insanely awful moments, I most certainly will survive.

# Thankful for Green Bean Casserole

Though my mom hosted massive Sunday dinners almost every week—filling our dining room to the brim with friends, family, neighbors, and our favorite foods—she preferred to keep Thanksgiving more intimate with only the family around the table. It was her favorite holiday. She decorated the table with cornucopias, little squash, and warm autumn colors, spending the day humming happily in the kitchen as she whipped up turkey, potatoes, and stuffing. I was always right at her heels, ready to help. Once around the table, we'd each share what we were thankful for that year.

My mother spent her last Thanksgiving in the hospital, but she wasn't about to miss out on her favorite holiday. Though bed-bound, she organized the entire menu, giving my dad, sisters and I detailed instructions for making the family traditional dishes.

We cooked everything at home and brought it to the hospital, spreading out the holiday meal in the waiting room. There, on the linoleum floor—among the plastic chairs that we knew all too well—we spread out turkey, mashed potatoes, stuffing, green bean casserole, cranberry sauce, gravy, and pumpkin pie. (We brought enough for the nurses, too). We helped my mom to the waiting room, and as we sat down, the normally cold and sterile space at once became warm and cozy. As always, we took turns sharing what we were grateful for that year. My mom wouldn't have had it any other way.

## The Thoughts:

1 can (10 oz.) Campbell's cream of mushroom soup
¾ c. milk
1 tsp. soy sauce
4 c. cooked cut green beans
1 ⅓ c. French's Original French Fried Onions
1 c. of Tradition

## Putting the Memory Together:

Mix soup and milk together in a 1 ½ quart baking dish. Stir in beans and half of the French fried onions Bake at 350 degrees for 30 minutes. Stir mixture and sprinkle on remaining onions. Bake for another 5 minutes, or until onions are golden brown. Remember to be thankful for all of the Thanksgiving dinners you have with you family.

Submitted by Emily Israel Hoffman, Chicago, IL.

# Angie's Selfless Sweets

These two delicious confections were favorites of my daughter Angie, who passed away from breast cancer in 2007 at the age of thirty-eight. She fought for nine years. Even as she battled, she was the kind of person who never sat still. She worked hard, started clubs, and volunteered one night a week at the Children's Memorial Hospital where she played with kids. She loved to cook, bake, and entertain and was always in the kitchen creating something delicious.

While undergoing chemotherapy, she often brought baked goods to the doctors and nurses—namely her famous brownies and chocolate snowballs. The doctors and nurses *loved* to see her walk in for an appointment. This was her way of thanking the wonderful people who cared for her with just the right mix of love and medicine. It made them feel good, it made her feel good, and it made us feel good. My sister loved to share her sweets, and she was very popular for it. We got great service—even nurses who weren't on her round would stop by!

I miss her terribly, but I can't help but smile when I think of her with these baked goods. I hope these recipes bring sunshine and joy to all who try them.

**Angie's Brownies**

**The Thoughts:**

½ c. butter

½ c. margarine

4 oz. unsweetened baking chocolate, melted

2 c. sugar

4 eggs

2 tsp. vanilla extract

1 c. flour

½ c. chocolate chips

1 bag Hershey's classic caramels

2 tsp. milk

A heaping cup of generosity

Sprinkle of energy to taste

**Putting the Memory Together:**

Melt chocolate with butter and margarine in saucepan over medium heat. Mix sugar, eggs (one at a time), and vanilla in large bowl. Add chocolate mixture to egg mixture and stir well. Stir in flour and chocolate chips. Pour into 9" x 12" pan sprayed with cooking spray. Bake at 350 degrees for twenty minutes. Do not over bake! Let brownies cool slightly. Meanwhile, make caramel topping. Unwrap caramels and place in microwave-safe bowl. Add milk. Microwave on high for thirty seconds and then stir. Repeat in fifteen seconds intervals until caramel is melted. Spread immediately on warm brownies. Bring to someone who least expects a treat and watch them smile.

**Angie's Chocolate Snowballs**

**The Thoughts:**

1 ½ c. semisweet chocolate chips
8 oz. cream cheese, cut into cubes
1 ½ tsp. vanilla extract
3 c. Oreo cookie crumbs
1 c. finely ground pecans (optional)
Powdered sugar for garnish
Top with selflessness
Sprinkle with love

**Putting the Memory Together:**

Melt chocolate chips in double boiler until smooth. Add cream cheese and vanilla, stirring until uniform. Remove from heat. Stir in cookie crumbs and pecans until thoroughly blended. Shape mixture into one inch balls and roll in powdered sugar. Cover and refrigerate eight hours or until firm, then roll in powdered sugar again. To store, refrigerate in airtight container. Serve to loved ones, especially those in need. Savor together, gathering strength from each other.

Submitted by Ronna Levy, Del Ray Beach, FL.

# 15-cent Risotto

In 1912, when my father was eleven years old, his family sent him from his home in Italy to live with an uncle in the United States. His family was supposed to be close behind, but when World War I broke out in Europe, they were unable to leave. Ultimately, they never joined my father. After the War, in attempt to disguise his Italian heritage, my father changed his name from Marco Antonio Lioni to Mark Anthony Lions.

In 1929, my father visited his family in Italy for the first time since his immigration. Once there, the Italian government declared that he must stay and serve in the Italian army. He escaped the country by walking to Austria, after which he returned to the United States.

My father stayed in the U.S. and started his own business making two-plate steel molds. He rarely kept in touch with his family, and didn't visit Italy again until 1973, when he traveled to his homeland with my mother, my husband, and I. On this trip, he saw his three brothers. Two had traveled from South America (where they fled after World War II), and one lived in Bolzano. They visited together for the first time since my father was eleven years old, and, after the reunion, they went their separate ways. All four passed away within the next ten years.

My father cooked dinner most Sunday nights, favoring Italian peasant food like polenta, rabbit stew, and venison. He even raised pigeons in a detached garage so we could eat squaw. One night, my father remembered that he used to eat this risotto, and he had a sudden craving. He called his cousin Mabel (who also lived in the U.S.) for the recipe. The long-distance phone call cost us fifteen cents. After we tasted it, we used to joke that it was the best fifteen cents he ever spent.

**The Thoughts:**

9 c. chicken broth (preferably homemade), warmed on stove

Olive oil

1 Tbsp. butter

Equal portions (about ⅓ c.) of finely chopped chicken giblets (gizzard, liver, and heart from a whole fryer)

⅓ c. Chopped onion

¼ c. Chopped parsley

3 c. uncooked Arborio rice

A pinch of salt and pepper

A spoonful of heritage

A dash of determination

**Putting the Memory Together:**

Before starting, get in touch with a relative or friend to talk about old times, preferably someone you haven't talked to in a long time. Next, coat a heavy-bottomed Dutch oven with oil. Add butter and melt until foaming stops. Add giblets, onion, and parsley and sauté until brown. Add rice and stir until slightly brown, scraping the brown bits from the bottom of the pan. Add one ladle of broth and stir well to further loosen the brown bits. Add another ladle of broth and cook until absorbed. Add additional broth—one or two ladles at a time—always stirring until absorbed before adding more broth. This is a labor of love that's not to be hurried. It will take at least thirty minutes until rice is cooked al dente. Add parmesan cheese and a bit more broth to make it soupy, if desired. Garnish with a blend of determination, pride, and renewed connection.

Submitted by Kathleen Anderson, Casselberry, FL.

# Enduring Sour Cream Coffee Cake

Sixty years ago, on September 12, my beautiful mother was the first American-born member of the Davidovitch family. She was born to parents who had survived Auschwitz and Dachau. Her family was so poor, when they first came to America her crib was a dresser drawer filled with hand-crocheted blankets.

Fifty years ago, my beautiful mom was a schoolgirl in Bensonhurst, Brooklyn, fluent in English and Yiddish and surrounded by friends and family.

Forty years ago, my beautiful mother attended a wedding where she met my father.

Thirty years ago, my mom was celebrating her 30th birthday as a mother of two, a committed wife, and the first college-educated member of her family.

Twenty years ago, my selfless mother was planning for the Bat Mitzvah of her only daughter.

Ten years ago, my mother was celebrating a son who graduated with an MBA and a daughter who graduated with honors and was dating the boy she would soon marry.

And ten years later, my mom celebrated her 60th birthday in a nursing home, stricken with Alzheimer's disease, unable to recognize her husband, daughter, or son.

While I have thousands of memories of my wonderful mother, many of them took place in the kitchen. I loved to watch her cook, to help her set the table for a holiday meal and to work side by side as we mixed, stirred, blended, whipped, and baked. Ever since I was old enough to help in the kitchen, my mom called me her "little helper" and her "little *balabusta*," which is Yiddish for "terrific homemaker." Every time we cooked together, my mom shared with me the story behind the dish—from whom it came and where she was the first time she tried it.

One of her oldest recipes was a sour cream coffee cake. The recipe survived the concentration camps and was passed down through many generations—from my great-grandmother to my grandmother, to my mother and, finally, to me. Sour cream coffee cake is a family favorite. I vividly remember walking home from the bus stop on crisp fall days and as soon as I turned the doorknob to come into the house, I smelled this fragrant, delicious cake. It smelled like home.

Tragic circumstances surrounded many generations of my mom's family. It's amazing how something as simple as coffee cake can bring a family together and encourage the passage of stories. My mom rarely talked about her parents' experience in the concentration camps, but each time we made this cake, I knew she was remembering her own mother and the days she spent cooking beside her. This simple coffee cake helps me keep my own mother's memory alive for my children, my children's children, for many generations to come.

## The Thoughts:

¼ c. brown sugar

¼ c. walnuts (optional)

2 tsp. cinnamon

3 c. flour

2 tsp. baking powder

2 tsp. baking soda

1 pint sour cream

½ lb. butter

2 c. sugar

4 eggs

1 tsp. vanilla extract

A pinch of sadness

A sprinkling of endurance

## Putting the Memory Together:

First, give a loving nickname to any other cooks in the kitchen. Next, preheat oven to 375 degrees. Mix brown sugar, cinnamon, and walnuts in a small bowl and set aside. Mix flour and baking powder and set aside. Mix baking soda with sour cream and set aside. Blend sugar and butter, then add eggs one at a time. Mix until cream in color. Alternate adding flour mixture and sour cream mixture until well blended. Stir in vanilla. Pour half of the batter into a greased bundt pan and sprinkle evenly with half of the brown sugar topping. Pour in the remaining batter, then top with remainder of the brown sugar mixture. Bake for one hour, or until a toothpick comes out clean. Let cool. Top with gratitude and a heaping portion of unshakeable courage. Before serving, savor the scent of home.

Submitted by Alissa Schor, Atlanta, GA.

# Mom's Step-by-Step Chocolate Chip Bundt Cake

Growing up, my mom's chocolate chip bundt cake was the centerpiece of every birthday, holiday, and family get-together. I can't recall a single special occasion when it didn't make an appearance. As much as I loved digging into that delicious cake, the ritual was always just as much fun.

My mother was a very methodical baker. She brought to her kitchen smiles and joy, of course, but also a very professional attitude. There was an order and process to everything. Attired in an apron, she would first clean the kitchen, giving herself plenty of room to work. Then, she would pull out the stepstools, so my sister and I could reach the counter and help pour ingredients into the bowl (I always liked to dump in extra chocolate chips). She would clean up as she went along, doing dishes and wiping down dirty surfaces. As soon as the cake went into the oven, there came our favorite part: fingers, hands, and faces in the bowl as we grabbed for beaters, spatulas, and anything else that had touched batter. The smell of the cake baking in the oven made our mouths water, and we would turn on the oven light and bend down to watch the cake rise. When it was finished, Mom would pull it out of the oven, let it cool, and dust it with powdered sugar. My favorite part has always been the outer layer, laden with (extra) chocolate chips.

Now that I have my own family, my wife and I continue to keep the tradition alive. My son just celebrated his first birthday and he had his very first taste of chocolate chip bundt cake. We still like to indulge in the licking of the bowl and beaters and spatulas, although my wife usually gets to it first (and leaves very little for me). The funniest part of this new tradition is the way it brings out our drastically different cooking styles: when my wife bakes, the kitchen is a mess; when I bake, there's an order and a process. I first clean the kitchen, giving myself plenty of room to work. I do the dishes and wipe down surfaces as I go along. It's just another way I keep my mom's memory alive.

## The Thoughts:

Crisco (or oil) and flour for pan
One package yellow cake mix
4 eggs, room temperature
1 c. sour cream, room temperature
1 packet vanilla instant pudding mix
½ c. vegetable oil
1 c. chocolate chips
1 Tbsp. Nestle Quick
1 Tbsp. sugar
Powdered sugar
1 c. tradition
1 tsp. anticipation
A sprinkle of process and order

## Putting the Memory Together:

Preheat oven to 350 degrees. Grease bundt pan with Crisco, then dust with flour (Cooking spray works too). Combine cake mix, eggs, sour cream, pudding mix, and oil. Beat on high for ten minutes. Wash used dishes. Combine chocolate chips, Nestle Quick, and sugar. Stir into sour cream mixture. Wash used dishes. Pour into bundt pan. Once settled, sprinkle in a few extra chocolate chips. Dig into batter immediately, keeping eyes peeled for batter thieves. Bake for fifty to fifty-five minutes, or until toothpick comes out clean. Wash used dishes and wipe down counters. Let cool completely before removing from pan. Dust with powdered sugar and serve with vanilla ice cream.

Submitted by Brian Kahn, Park City, UT.

# Max's Chavetah

My father, Max Michelson, was born in the United States. When he was young, his parents died in a typhoid epidemic, so he ended up the foster child of a wealthy English couple in Israel, the Longos, who lived in the original colony of Zichron Yaakov.

My parents were childhood sweethearts. They met at school, and even when my father became captain of the Israeli soccer team and played all over the world, he always loved my mother. As a young man, his parents sent him to Mikveh Israel agricultural college, where he majored in beekeeping. His foster mother grew sick and the Longos sent my father to the U.S., telling him that the future was in America. My father's grandfather lived there as well, so he was not alone. He traveled overseas and set up a home in Chicago. While he was away, Mrs. Longo passed away. Shortly after, Mr. Longo was found dead on his wife's grave after suffering a self-inflicted gunshot wound.

All this time, my father continued to write love letters to my mother. He saved his money in the hope of marrying her and bringing her to the U. S. After two years, he returned to Israel and approached my mother's family. They were married and they returned to the U.S. shortly after. They lived together until my dad passed away in 1973. They were always meant for each other.

My dad was a master chavetah maker. His signature chavetah, similar to an omelet, was made with onions (typically Israeli), and I always considered myself lucky when he made one for me. Fine by itself, but with fresh bread and an Israeli salad, it's a feast!

Editor's Note: please see Belinda Brock's Israeli Salad recipe.

## The Thoughts:

2 or 3 large eggs, beaten
1 Tbsp. water
½ onion, minced
1-1 ½ Tbsp. butter (or combination of oil and butter)
Salt and freshly ground pepper, to taste
A sprinkle of adventure
A teaspoon of commitment
Destiny to taste

## Putting the Memory Together:

Sauté onions in butter over medium heat, stirring occasionally until brown. If necessary, add more oil or butter to coat pan, then add the eggs. Cook without stirring, occasionally lifting edge of chavetah and tipping pan to let uncooked egg mixture run to the edges (It takes some wrist action). When eggs are nearly set, flip the chavetah in the air and finish cooking the second side over medium-low heat. Note: Chavetah is flat, not folded (like a French omelet), and cooked on both sides. Serve to those you love and have always loved.

Submitted by Belinda Brock, Highland Park, IL.

# Traditional Israeli Salad

My mother's family was one of the original founding families of Israel. Her father was one of thirteen men to receive a plot of land from Baron Rothschild. They owned more than one-hundred acres in Zichron Yaakov, one of the original colonies. They grew grapes which Baron Rothschild bought and made into wine. These small beginnings eventually grew into the Carmel winery.

It was a wonderfully warm community. When my mother was born, the neighbors became quasi-midwives, and everyone came over to help. By the time the doctor arrived, she was already born. When her family needed anything—oranges, avocados, or grapefruit they turned to their friends and neighbors and traded grapes. My mom grew up eating only wonderful, natural food. They didn't use artificial sweeteners or order pizzas—everything was grown by people she knew and loved.

This is the recipe that all of my family members mention when talking about my mom. It's the quintessential Israeli dish, as much today as ever, yet it is simple to make and uses only a few fresh ingredients. Accordingly, my mom always bought the best vegetables, particularly tomatoes, which have to be ripe, but firm. Part of what's distinctive about this salad is that the vegetables are cut into tiny pieces. The small cubes remain crunchy and flavorful even as salt makes them release their juices, creating a delicious mix that's perfect for dunking bread. In Israel, it is not unusual to eat this salad for breakfast.

## The Thoughts:

4 tomatoes, diced
1 onion, diced
4 pickling cucumbers, peeled and diced
Juice of one lemon
1-2 Tbsp. extra-virgin olive oil
Salt and freshly ground pepper to taste
A sprinkle of tradition
Neighborly love to taste

## Putting the Memory Together:

Head to a farmer's market or turn to your own backyard, if you're a gardener and select the freshest vegetables you can find. Mix diced veggies in a bowl with oil and lemon juice. Add seasonings to taste. Serve cold or at room temperature, for breakfast, lunch, or dinner. Make extra and pass to friends and neighbors in exchange for homegrown or homemade treats. Enjoy with family. Note: Some add red pepper, parsley, mint, or even radishes Green onions can also be substituted for white.

Submitted by Belinda Brock, Highland Park, IL.

# Christel's Magic Christmas Cake

When I was little, we would spend every Christmas Day at my grandparents' place. I would crawl underneath the side table in their living room, disappearing completely beneath the crochet lace tablecloth. In my little hidey hole, I was in my own world. I would play detective (eavesdropping on the adult enemies' conversations), sing self-composed songs and indulge my imagination. But my favorite thing to do was listen to the stories my Opa would tell about the days when he and my Oma were young and and beautiful.

Every Christmas, my Opa would pull out the story of how he and my Oma met, during the war in December, 1942. She was a young, pretty nurse in medical school, he was a proud assistant doctor who became "weak at his knees" at the mere sight of her. According to my Opa (and this is the part he directed towards me in a whisper), he did not so much fall in love with my Oma's blonde locks and good looks as he did with her "magic" Christmas cake, which was filled with "the taste of love" that sparked their romance and eventually developed into a beautiful love story.

Maybe it was the fact that this story was a crucial chapter in my family's history, or maybe it was the magic and "the taste of love" in my Oma's cake, but I remember the incredible sense of safety each time I heard my grandparents' tale. My little potbelly, the result of eating too much of the warm cake's custard filling too fast, would comfortably ache in agreement. After my Oma passed away, her recipe book became a way for me to remember her and keep her in my life. Just as I can't imagine my life without both of my grandparents, I can no longer imagine my life without making the "magic" cake each Christmas, recalling the story of how my Opa and Oma fell in love, and remembering how they shaped me into the person I am today.

There are but a handful of moments in our life that truly stay with us for the rest of our days. Amongst mine are those that relate to my grandparents: bittersweet memories filled with glee, comfort, and a pleasant belly ache over my Opa's stories and my Oma Christel's magic Christmas cake.

**The Thoughts:**

Cake:

⅓ c. all-purpose flour
⅓ c. self-rising flour
4 eggs, separated
⅔ c. caster sugar
1 tsp vanilla extract
4 Tbsp. hot water
A heaping taste of love
A sprinkling of magic

Custard/orange filling:

1 c. milk
¼ c. whipping cream
1 vanilla bean, split lengthways, seeds lightly scraped
5 large egg yolks
⅓ c. superfine sugar
1 orange
½ c. margarine
A dash of safety

Icing:

2 c. powdered sugar, sifted
½ tsp. vanilla
Lemon juice
3-5 tsp. warm water

**Putting the Memory Together:**

Preheat oven to 350 degrees. Grease and line two 8" x 8"cake pans. Sift flours three times to aerate and set aside. Beat egg whites till soft peaks form. Gradually mix in sugar and vanilla, beating well after each addition. Beat for five more minutes or until sugar dissolves and mixture is thick, pale, and tripled in volume. Use a spatula to gently fold in egg yolks, then flour and water. Divide batter between prepared pans. Bake fifteen to twenty minutes or until cake springs back when lightly touched. Turn cakes onto a tea towel and upturn onto wire rack and allow to cool.

While cake cools, pull out a few classic stories—especially family tales that go way back in time. Peel and slice the orange into small pieces and spread evenly on one sponge cake. Make custard by heating the milk, cream, and vanilla pod and seeds in a heavy saucepan over medium heat until just below boiling. Remove from heat. Whisk egg yolks and sugar in a bowl until well combined. Gradually whisk hot milk mixture into the yolk mixture and return to the same pan over medium-low heat. Stir gently and continuously with a wooden spoon, reaching the base and corners, for four to five minutes until the custard is thick enough to coat the back of the spoon. Remove from heat and strain through a fine sieve into a container, discarding the vanilla pod. Let margarine melt, spoon by spoon, into warm custard. Cool custard-margarine mix for ten to fifteen minutes, stirring occasionally to prevent a skin from forming. Spoon warm custard-margarine mix over orange pieces and cover with other cake. To make icing, whisk all ingredients together until smooth. Drizzle over cake and serve dusted with additional powdered sugar. Best eaten while custard is still warm. Overindulge until you have that warm, safe, comfortable, and slightly achy feeling in your belly!

Submitted by: Anya Weimann, Sydney, Australia

# Dave's Baked Beans

Growing up, my mom was usually the cook in the family. We were fortunate she was able to stay at home for most of our school-age years while our dad worked outside the home. Thus, Mom cooked us dinner every night when we came home from school, ballet class, or sports practice and whipped up the occasional big breakfast on the weekends. Mom certainly had her specialties, and her cooking was filled with reliable, traditional dishes that we still share as a family today.

While Mom's dishes were the edible thread through our daily lives, Dad was manned the grill or oven on holidays. Dad's turkey graced our table on Thanksgiving, his ham was the centerpiece of the Easter table, and his burgers and dogs were the highlight of Fourth of July. Over the years, Dad's dishes became special occasion celebrities due to their annual appearance on our table. One of Dad's most celebrated dishes (celebrated not only by our immediate family, but the extended family as well) was his baked beans, which usually emerged for Easter or Father's Day. They were always served in the same mustard-colored porcelain bowl. Over time, it became known as the "bean bowl." He was an accountant with a methodical way of doing things, and would often set the bean bowl out the night before, building our anticipation for the delicious baked beans. Arrival at many a family gathering was greeted with an inquiry into the whereabouts of "Dave's Beans." No questions were required once they saw the bean bowl.

Sadly, my dad was diagnosed with inoperable lung cancer the Easter before I graduated from college. He passed away only six months later, and it took my mom, sister and me at least one round of holidays before we were able to face our family traditions without the man who made so many of them happen.

We attempted Dad's beans one of the following Easters, but they weren't quite the same without him there to set them proudly on the table. Occasionally, we'll still make a batch of Dave's Beans, but I'm convinced he had a special touch that none of us can replicate, as they never taste quite as good. Almost ten years have passed since we lost Dad, but whenever I'm at my mom's house and happen to open the cabinet with the mustard-colored porcelain bowl, I'm immediately comforted by the memory and taste of his special baked beans.

**The Thoughts:**

1 pkg. dried baby lima beans (preferably Goya)
1 pkg. bacon or the equivalent amount of salt pork
1 can tomato soup (preferably Campbell's)
3 heaping spoonfuls of molasses
Salt to taste
A dose of expectation
A spoonful of tradition
A very particular serving dish

**Putting the Memory Together:**

Pull out the chosen bowl the night before and set on the counter to let family know what's coming. Rinse beans in cold water and soak in the baking bowl overnight. The next morning, bring beans and water just to a boil, adding a pinch of salt. Dice bacon (or salt pork), reserving a few pieces for the top. Add diced bacon to bean bowl, greasing the sides as you go. Remove beans from cooking broth and add to bacon. Add tomato soup, one can of cooking broth, and molasses. Stir well. Top with reserved bacon or salt pork strips. Cover with foil. Bake at 325 degrees for three to three and a half hours, removing foil after the first one and a half to two hours to allow top to crisp. Enjoy with those you love!

Submitted by Alison Stankus, Chicago, IL.

# Grandma Anna's Gefilte Fish

My Grandma Anna cooked her gefilte fish for Passover and Rosh Hashanah every year in her apartment in Far Rockaway, New York. She immigrated to New York from Russia in 1922 following the pogroms. That year, when Cossack soldiers came to her door, they began shooting her entire family. Both her parents died that day, but somehow, without being seen by the soldiers, Anna's sister Ruchel instructed her to lie down and pretend she was dead. They were both spared.

Shortly thereafter, Anna married Ben Schwartz, as had been arranged by their families (Ben's family sold wheat, and Anna's family owned a mill). They immigrated to the United States, crossing the sea with their newly born infant, Frances. My grandma never talked about that loss in her life. To my sisters and me, she was the warmest, sweetest grandmother imaginable. She and my grandfather worked hard at their Rockaway fruit store and took the bus every week to visit my family on Long Island. She always came with something, cookies she had baked, a bargain she had picked up in the "willage" (her version of the village, or downtown Rockaway) or some treasure she had found.

As she aged, we began to worry that the gefilte fish recipe would be lost forever. My sister Judy went to her apartment and watched closely as she made it. Since no written recipe existed (and Grandma Anna had no notion of measuring the quantities), Judy took the ingredients from Grandma's hands before they went into the bowl, measuring each with standard spoons and cups. In this way, Grandma Anna will always live on.

**The Thoughts:**

½ lb. ground carp

2 lb. ground whitefish

1 lb. ground trout

2 lb. onions, chopped fine

3-4 tbsp. vegetable or canola oil

4 eggs

1-2 tsp. freshly ground black pepper

¾ c. matzo meal

4 carrots, peeled and cut in half

2-3 tsp. salt

1 ½ tsp. sugar

A heaping cupful of courage

A sprinkle of determination

A teaspoon of positivity

Note: When you ask the fishmonger to grind the fish for you, request that they set aside the bones, skins, and heads to include in your order.

**Putting the Memory Together:**

Sauté onions in a large sauté pan. In a large bowl, combine fish with one eighth of the onions, eggs, and black pepper. Add matzo meal and salt. Add one third to one half a cup of water and sugar to the fish mixture. If it seems too loose, add another one eight cup of matzo meal. In a very large pot, place carrots, remaining onions, a teaspoon of salt, a teaspoon of sugar, more pepper, fish bones, and heads. Add water to cover and bring to a boil. Form balls from ground fish mixture with your hands and add them gently to the pot. If liquid level is not covering the balls, add water. Adjust stove temperature so the liquid is simmering. Place fish skins on top of mixture in pot. Cover and cook for one and a half hours, then cook uncovered for thirty minutes. When fish is cooked, allow mixture to cool and gently remove the fish balls and place into a container. Strain the fish broth. When broth is fully cooled, spoon enough over fish balls to keep moist and refrigerate. Remaining broth can be frozen for later use. Reserve cooked carrots in separate container and discard bones, heads, and skins.

To serve: Bring gefilte fish to room temperature. Place a piece of lettuce on a plate. Place fish on top and garnish with cherry tomatoes and a few slices of cooked carrot. Serve with horseradish.

Submitted by: Denise Davis, Highland Park, IL.

# Shirley's Perfectly Frozen Apple Pie

My mother, Shirley Shapiro, was an amazing pie maker. She had all the qualities of a good cook and baker: creativity, patience, and attention to detail. But what separated her from the pack was the love she infused into every cooking project. She cooked purely to make those she loved happy, and pies were her specialty. Apple, blueberry, cherry, rhubarb—they were all baked with only the freshest ingredients. I can still remember her with her rolling pin and apron, working in the kitchen intensely molding the edges of the crust.

In the fall of 1990, my wife, Robin, and my daughters, Lauren and Brittany, had been over at my parents' house for dinner, where we had savored one of Mom's famous apple pies for dessert. As we were leaving, Mom placed something in my hands: an apple pie for the freezer. It was heavy in my hands, as it was wrapped, double-wrapped, and triple-wrapped to withstand a nuclear war. It came with a complete set of preparation instructions, for when we were ready to indulge.

She handed me a separate container filled with the sugary streusel topping and labeled 10/31/90. A note card read: *Place apple filling in foil. Top apple with streusel topping. Bake 425 degrees for 15 minutes, then reduce to 350 and bake until apples are "fork tender."* My mother rarely left things to chance.

Just about six months later, my family and I were on vacation in Palm Springs when we got a call from my parents. Mom had been diagnosed with colon cancer. Though she was a nurse and my father was a physician, they had spent all of their time caring for others. My mother had never gone for a colonoscopy, and now it was too late. Just a few months later, my mother passed away at the age of seventy-five.

We had been saving that apple pie, and once my mom got sick, our minds were elsewhere. After she passed, it never seemed to be the right time. We just kept it and kept it, hoping the triple wrapping would keep the apple pie secure. Even ten years later, the pie is still in the freezer. I just can't bring myself to eat it.

**The Thoughts:**

Crust:

1 pastry crust for a 9-inch, deep-dish pie (homemade or store bought)

Filling:

½ c. sugar
3 Tbsp. all-purpose flour
1 tsp. ground cinnamon
⅛ tsp. salt
6 c. thinly sliced and peeled apples (a mix of Golden Delicious and Fuji is preferred)

Streusel Topping:

½ c. flour
½ c. brown sugar
4 Tbsp. butter
1 tsp. Cinnamon (optional)
½ c. chopped pecans (optional)
A great working freezer

**Putting the Memory Together:**

Crust:

Prepare your homemade or store-bought crust. (Editor's note: For a homemade recipe, please see Enid Barnes' "Mom's Perfect Pie Crust.")

Filling:

Preheat oven to 375 degrees. In a mixing bowl, stir together the sugar, flour, cinnamon and salt. Add apple slices and gently toss until coated. Transfer apple mixture to pie shell. Bake for about fifty minutes.

Streusel Topping:

Combine flour and sugar in food processor. Cut in butter. Add pecans if desired. Sprinkle evenly over just-baked pie. Bake for an additional twelve minutes. Enjoy. If you are lucky enough to have leftovers, freeze them for up to ten years!

Submitted by Donald Shapiro, Northbrook, IL.

# Grammie O's Holiday Jell-O Mold

Growing up, one of my favorite times of the year was Thanksgiving because it brought my whole family together. My parents came from completely different backgrounds, so each set of grandparents had a totally different idea about what Thanksgiving dinner should be. My father grew up on a farm in Arkansas where my grandmother cooked everything from scratch. My mother grew up in a tiny Chicago suburb. Her father was a prominent attorney, and her family often ordered out or had a cook come to their house. In our combination of Thanksgiving customs, my maternal grandmother would sit at the head of the table delegating tasks and ringing a bell to summon us all to the table. Meanwhile my paternal grandfather would hear the bell, jump up and think, "Oh, great! My dish is ready to serve!" Because they were so different, it worked. They loved and appreciated each other for the people they were.

Thanksgiving dinner always included my paternal grandmother's cranberry Jell-O mold. Every year, I would sit in the kitchen while my grandmother prepared it. Because it was such an intricate recipe, we were able to spend more time together. In addition to my job as designated grape slicer, my grandmother also gave me the role of taster. I would try the Jell-O mold throughout its various stages, waiting anxiously for the last step of the recipe, when I got to sample the delicious pineapple topping. This annual moment in the kitchen with my grandmother taught me to love cooking.

**The Thoughts:**

Mold Filling:

2 c. sugar
1 lb. fresh cranberries
2 boxes raspberry Jell-O
1 Tbsp. Knox gelatin
1 lb. Tokay red grapes, sliced in half
1 c. crushed pineapple
1 c. crushed pecans
A dash of city
A pinch of country

Topping:

1 c. crushed pineapple
1 small box vanilla pudding mix
¾ of a brick of cream cheese, softened
1 Dream Whip package, prepared

**Putting the Memory Together:**

To make filling, grind cranberries in food processor and stir in two cups of sugar. Refrigerate overnight. Dissolve Jell-O in two cups of hot water. Add Knox gelatin and, once dissolved, add one and a half cups cold water. Get the seal of approval from the taster. Add cranberry mixture and remaining ingredients and refrigerate until firm.

To make the topping, mix all ingredients in large bowl. Once combined and approved by the taster, spread over set filling and refrigerate. Top with love and appreciation. Assemble a gathering of people from very different backgrounds, and serve.

Submitted by Carrie Ratliff, Chicago, IL.

# Sunday Morning Golden Puff Donuts

Every Sunday morning when I was growing up, I would wake to the smell of frying bacon. The aroma would hit my nose as I lay in bed, alerting me to the fact that it was almost 7:30 and my mom, Mavis Miller, would soon be calling my brother, sister, and I down to breakfast. The table would be covered with made-from-scratch biscuits, bacon, and fresh eggs.

Everything changed my freshman year of high school when I brought home a recipe from my Home Economics class. I told my mom we *had* to make these donuts. She wasn't too keen on the idea, especially because Dad was reluctant to try new things. But she agreed to make them anyway, and Dad completely surprised us when he loved them—so much so that at least one Sunday every month, Mom added donuts to our Sunday breakfast menu. My sister and I loved to help, filling a Ziploc with powdered sugar and shaking the hot donuts until they were deliciously covered. Even after I grew up and left our central Illinois farmhouse, my mom would still make donuts on my visits home—on the condition that I help by shaking the donuts in the Ziploc bag. Of course, I was happy to oblige!

**The Thoughts:**

3 c. canola oil for frying
2 c. flour
¼ c. granulated sugar
3 tsp. baking powder
1 tsp. salt
¼ c. canola oil
¾ c. milk
1 tsp. vanilla extract
1 egg
Powdered sugar
A pinch of persuasion
A portion of family teamwork

**Putting the Memory Together:**

Heat canola oil in deep fryer or 1-quart saucepan to about 375 degrees. Mix together flour, sugar, baking powder, and salt. Add oil, milk, vanilla, and egg. Stir with fork until thoroughly mixed. Drop teaspoons of dough into hot oil, frying four to five at a time. Cook about three minutes, turning to brown on all sides. Alongside loved ones, place donuts in Ziploc bag filled with powdered sugar and shake until well coated. Serve on Sunday mornings, or whenever children return to the nest.

Submitted by: Sherry Simpson, Valparaiso, IN.

# McFadden's Game Day Chili

My dad, Victor McFadden, was not only the first McFadden on this side of the pond to go to college, he was also a "Double Domer"— someone with two degrees from Notre Dame. He married my mom, Bonnie, while he was at Notre Dame, and though the school was all male at that time, they lived together in a section of student housing for married veterans (My dad fought in Korea). Every Saturday during football season, my mom would cook a big pot of chili, and the single male students, as well as their married neighbors, would come over to hang out before heading to the stadium together.

After seven years in what they called "Vet Ville," my mom and dad moved to another house before finally settling into a two-story white home just blocks from the Notre Dame campus. The game day tradition established in "Vet Ville" continued. Their prime location meant that family, friends, and former Domers would drop by before games (some coming in from out of town, forcing my brothers and me to give up our rooms), and my mom always had an enormous pot of chili on the stove. We'd hang out in the backyard as the season began, later moving inside as temperatures dropped, and walk to the stadium in big groups. The house would often fill up post-game too, and my mom would either start another pot of chili or whip up a delicious spread of snacks.

Even now, though my dad has been gone for several years, folks still find their way to my mother's house, where they'll always find a pot of chili and a crew of fellow Notre Dame fans.

**The Thoughts:**

1 lb. ground beef

1 medium onion, chopped

2 (15 oz.) cans red beans, undrained (not chili beans)

4 (10 oz.) cans tomato soup

Chili powder

A pinch of salt

A dash of pepper

Cheese and sour cream, for serving

A heaping portion of game day excitement

**Putting the Memory Together:**

Brown ground beef with onion. Add salt and pepper to taste. Stir in red beans, soup and as much chili powder as your tongue will allow. Let simmer for thirty minutes, stirring often, so it doesn't burn. Serve with cheese and sour cream on the side and don't forget a heaping spoonful of team spirit! Best eaten with a crowd of fellow super fans.

Submitted by Maureen McFadden, South Bend, IN.

# Camp Ojibwa Poppy Seed Cake

My big brother, Eric, was the roughest, toughest, boldest little boy ever. He was an adventurous sports fanatic, and every summer, he and my other older brother Jason would head up to Ojibwa Camp in Eagle River, Wisconsin, for eight weeks. There, Eric and Jason took their love of sports to a whole new level, participating in every athletic event Ojibwa offered. Eric was a natural athlete who brought a competitive drive to everything he did. Ojibwa was truly his time to shine.

As much as the boys looked forward to their first day of camp, I looked forward to the intermission between session one and two, when families were invited to spend a four day weekend with the campers in Eagle River. Things were really quiet without my rambunctious older brothers at home, and I was always excited to load into the mini-van with my parents and grandparents to hang out with my brothers and their cute friends. We would pull into the parking lot and wait for the campers in a big grassy field. My brothers would come running out from the cabins with huge smiles on their faces, their hair messy, their clothes a little dirty from a month at camp. During the days, we would take the boys to town and dine out or hang out at camp and play games with the other families. At night, we would drop them back off at the cabins and spend the night at a hotel.

For each trip, my mom would pack bags of games, snacks, clothing, and surprises for the boys. As excited as Eric was to see his family, we all knew he was really excited about the freshly baked poppy seed cake made by our close family friend, Cheryl Levi. Eric just loved seeds: he was always spitting sunflower seeds all over his room. Though the two of us fought when we were young—my mom used to call us "oil and water"—I secretly loved the attention from my big brother. As we grew up, our tumultuous sibling relationship matured into true friendship. This cake will always remind me of those summers together.

**The Thoughts:**

1 box Pillsbury yellow cake mix
1 pkg. lemon pudding mix
1 c. water
½ c. oil
4 eggs
4 Tbsp. poppy seeds
A pinch of adventure

**Putting the Memory Together:**

Soak poppy seeds in water for thirty minutes. Mix cake and pudding mixes and then add water, poppy seeds, and oil. Beat in eggs one at a time. Coat bundt pan with non-stick spray and pour in batter. Bake at 350 degrees for forty-five minutes. Cool fifteen minutes on wire rack. Serve with a side of rough and a topping of tumble. Best eaten in the great outdoors.

Submitted by Marissa Eson, Chicago, IL.

# Pearl Harbor Chicken

My mother died of pneumonia when I was five months old. My dad was in the army, so my aunt stepped in to take care of my brother and me. When I was four years old, we were sent over on a huge boat to live with my dad in Hawaii, where he was stationed at Trippler General Hospital.

One day after we moved into his home on Fort Shaft, I was getting ready for Sunday school. I was putting on my best dress and my patent leather shoes when I looked out the window and said, "Gee, it looks like a war out there!" From our home on the hill, we could see the big, round oil barrels bursting, exploding into the air. We had no idea what was happening, but shortly after, the military police came to our door and herded everyone from our area into a radio tunnel and then into a huge radio room. Men with guns guarded the doors outside. The room was crowded, and we couldn't drink any of the water for fear of it being poisoned. We drank juice instead. We slept two people to a cot. Four women actually had their babies while we waited in that room. A week later, we were allowed to return to our homes, but things were anything but normal. We had to wear our life preservers all the time and we had regular drills to get out to the boat quickly.

Because my dad was in the service, we didn't have many traditional family meals or customs, but we always went to the Officer's Club for lunch on holidays or special days where we'd enjoy a large spread. On those special occasions, my stepmother always made a roast chicken, and we'd make chicken sandwiches for dinner.

**The Thoughts:**

1 whole chicken
¾ c. olive oil
A dash of salt
A pinch of pepper
A teaspoon of history

**Putting the Memory Together:**

Preheat oven to 325 degrees. Remove giblets from chicken and trim away any loose skin. Rinse chicken in cold water and pat dry with a paper towel. Place chicken, breast side up, in a roasting pan with sides at least 1-inch high. Rub the chicken with olive oil. Salt and pepper inside and outside of the bird. You may also add lemon juice, chicken broth, or fresh herbs to season. Place the roasting pan on an oven rack in the lower-middle part of the oven. Roast the chicken for sixty minutes or until juices run clear. Remove from oven, cover with foil, and let rest for fifteen minutes before carving. Garnish with bravery, sprinkle with gutsiness, and serve with family endurance.

Submitted by Jane Santana, Zion, IL.

# Havana Flan

Growing up in Cuba, the kitchen in our house was always filled with pots and pans. My mother had different pans for every kind of food: meat, rice, and lots of fish. Every morning, she went to the mercado to pick up live fish, lobster, or my favorite, red snapper. She cooked the fish whole, always using the perfect amount of seasoning.

I had ten brothers and sisters. At dinnertime, we all took turns washing our hands and faces. My father wouldn't start dinner until we were all there, lined up on benches between my father and mother, who sat on chairs at the heads of the table.

Nearly every meal ended with dessert. My favorite was flan, which my mother made every Sunday and Thursday. She would often add fruit like mango or arraba. We would pick the fruit from our own trees and bring it in to her. In 1952, when I was thirty-three years old, I came to America where an abundance of ready-made confections made it easy to stop making my own desserts. But flan will always remind me of my mother.

**The Thoughts:**

¾ c. white sugar

8 oz. cream cheese, softened

5 eggs

14 oz. can sweetened condensed milk

12 oz. can evaporated milk

1 tsp. vanilla

Mangos

**Putting the Memory Together:**

Preheat oven to 350 degrees. In a small, heavy saucepan, cook sugar over medium-low heat, stirring until golden. Pour into 10-inch round baking dish and set aside. In a large bowl, beat cream cheese until smooth. Beat in eggs one at a time. Beat in condensed and evaporated milk and vanilla until smooth. Pour into the caramel coated pan. Line a roasting pan with a damp kitchen towel. Place baking dish on towel inside roasting pan, and place on oven rack. Fill roasting pan half full of boiling water. Bake for fifty minutes, or until center is set. Cool one hour and then refrigerate for at least eight hours. Garnish with sliced mangos that have been sprinkled with sugar. Best served at a big ole' table with the entire family clean and present.

Submitted by Victoria Bello, Havana, Cuba/Chicago, IL.

# Chapter 2

## Connecting through Nurturing

**"Sharing food with another human being is an intimate act that should not be indulged in lightly." —M.F.K. Fisher**

After my mother's death, I felt utterly alone. From home to work and back home again, I moved like a zombie, coming out of my coma only to cook dinner for my father. I kept our home afloat, but inside I was drowning. Even as time passed—and even after my one month stint at a grief center in California—I felt isolated from the rest of the world. My friends would complain about their mothers and I would think, "Well, at least you have a Mom." I felt like since my mom was gone, the people around me couldn't understand my life. I was floating along this ebbing, flowing river of grief completely on my own.

It wasn't until I reconnected with an old friend who had lost her father that I felt like someone *got* me. She knew the feeling of envy I had when I saw a mother and daughter walking down the street together. She could sympathize with my inability to get out of bed some days. She understood my panic when I would realize—again and again—that my mom wasn't there to answer a question about a recipe or to remind me of her no fail fever remedy. Conversations with this friend warmed my soul. I was buoyed by a feeling of hope that I couldn't find elsewhere. Our connection narrowed what seemed like a gap between me and the rest of the world. At the end of our conversations, I would feel like I could breathe. I was comforted, as though the wound of my mother's death was at least beginning to form a scab. Connecting with this friend provided a salve I hadn't yet known.

I found the scab continued to heal when I was able to connect with the memory of my mother. After she had been gone for two years, I began to struggle, unable to get in touch with the small details that I was desperate to remember. What did her lotion smell like? What were her expressions at particular moments? What did her perfectly polished fingernails and delicate hands look like? I was shocked at how quickly those details faded from my mind, a common affliction among those who have lost a loved one. But when I began to cook her foods regularly, everything changed. Just one whiff of her baked apples, and I could see the two of us, settled in at my kitchen table after school, chatting about my day. A bite of stuffed peppers, and I was instantly in the grocery store, pushing the cart while she tossed in ingredients. The feel of bread dough in my hands, and we were together in the kitchen, preparing Sunday night dinner side by side. Every night, when I would start to cook, I would be inundated with vivid memories of my mother.

"Our senses connect us intimately to the past, connect us in ways that most of our cherished ideas never could," says Diane Ackerman in *A Natural History of the Senses*. I found this to be true: the sights, smells, sounds, and tastes of the kitchen flawlessly connected me to her memory in a vibrant, detailed way that didn't happen when I tried to piece images together in my mind. I relished these memories, turning to her recipes when I needed to be nurtured.

For thousands of years, human beings have used food to nurture both themselves and others. We slurp up chicken noodle soup when we're sick. We turn to comfort foods, like macaroni and cheese, when we're sad. We bring casseroles when someone has passed away. While food naturally fills a physical emptiness, making us un-hungry, it also satisfies an emotional void. It nurtures us, even more so when the foods have an emotional connotation—evoking powerful memories through smells, tastes, even the mere sight of them. It is these memory evoking meals that often become coping mechanisms for survivors after a death.

Amazingly, food provides another mode of comfort: it brings people together. In the wake of death, leaning on friends and family for support becomes crucial, and food becomes the unifying element. As we use culinary talents to nurture ourselves and those around us, we strengthen bonds, tighten relationships, and foster our connections to family and friends. It's a beautiful moment when we connect simultaneously with others and with the person we've lost. It intensifies the link to both parties, nurturing both past and present relationships. I found that when I was gathered with my family and friends, indulging in one of my mother's classic dishes, grief began to take a backseat. Without even making the conscious decision, we were celebrating her life instead. Our happiness, not our grief.

Like so many others, I feel especially lonely for my mom around the holidays, or when we have a big family event coming up. But it's during this time that I find myself most nurtured. As we plan for our holiday gatherings, I find myself on the phone with my two sisters daily, determining who is bringing what dish and calling each other with recipe questions. The day of the big dinner, we gather in my kitchen to slice, dice, chop, and heat, putting the finishing touches on the dishes that mom used to make. As sweet smells float thorough my oven-warmed kitchen, we share our favorite stories about mom. We laugh, we cry, we talk, and as we nurture ourselves with food and memories made infinitely more vivid by the smells and tastes of her dishes, we connect with each other and the memory of our mother. It doesn't necessarily fill the vast, dark void left by her absence, but it helps make it a little lighter. If my mom were alive today, I know that she would savor the sight of her three daughters together in the kitchen, nurturing their relationships with conversation and their bodies with comforting food. To me, that honors her memory in the best way possible.

In this chapter, you'll find stories about connecting and nurturing. In each submission, food plays a central role in bringing people together. Whether the story takes place during a loved one's life or is a part of the grieving journey after they had passed, these dishes serve up a way of connecting, both with the lost loved one and with those still present. In both realms, a dash of connection nurtures the survivor inside and out. The void left by the deceased will never be filled, but the warmth of memories whisked together with the glow of affectionate relationships offers a lovely comfort that can make the emptiness feel a little less vast.

# Grandma Elaine's Diva-licious Tuna and Egg Salad

Grandma Elaine was a character. She had a cozy two-bedroom apartment in Miami Beach, where she lived the life of a retired Hollywood starlet. She had gorgeous skin (despite years in the sun), smelled like a combination of Ponds cold cream and Oil of Olay lotion, and had long, red, round fingernails that would click on the piano when she played. She was always the star of the show, out on the town every night, in the center of every photo and—regardless of her age—always gawked at by gentlemen, which she loved. She would walk around the house in big, boldly printed muumuus, carefreely inging, "Que Sera Sera," stopping only to yell at my sisters and I to put on lipstick—but only if it was red or hot pink.

I suppose that Grandma Elaine was a bit of a hoarder. She had little decorative trinkets all over her house, and there were change purses tucked everywhere—in drawers, closets, under mattresses, even in kitchen cupboards. They were all full of money, since she tended to hide all of her spare cash in hopes that her kids would slip her a few extra bucks when they were in town.

Money wasn't the only thing she hid. As a kid, going to Grandma Elaine's was a treat, because there was candy hidden *everywhere*. She had a crazy sweet tooth, but because her kids and her doctors had instructed her to eliminate junk food from her diet, she hid huge candy bars all over the kitchen. At any given moment, you could open a cabinet to pull out a water glass and come face to face with a chunk of a Hershey's bar, or open the silverware drawer for a fork and find three miniature Kit-Kats instead. Visiting Grandma Elaine was like a junk food treasure hunt, and we loved every minute of it.

Of course, we couldn't just eat candy, so Grandma Elaine always made us delicious lunches. We would all sit in the kitchen, and she would pull out a big chopping bowl and toss together all the ingredients for egg or tuna salad. She was an eye-baller, so she would mix it all together effortlessly, almost as though she was doing it in her sleep. Then she would serve it to us on white bread, and we would watch game shows or old black-and-white movies, with the television turned up as loud as it would go.

**The Thoughts:**

Tuna Salad
2 (7 oz.) cans of white albacore tuna fish
½ c. mayonnaise
1 c. chopped celery
¼ c. chopped onion
2 hard boiled eggs, chopped
½ tsp. salt
1 tube of red lipstick

**Putting the Memory Together:**

Drain tuna and break into small pieces. Combine all ingredients, mix lightly, and sing "Que Sera Sera."

Egg Salad
6 large hard boiled eggs, chopped
2 stalks celery, chopped
¼ c. chopped onion
2 Tbsp. mayonnaise
½ tsp. salt
½ tsp. pepper
1 black-and-white movie

**Putting the Memory Together:**

Combine all ingredients, mix lightly, and serve. Take a family photo to capture the beauty of something as mundane as egg salad.

Submitted by Emily Israel Hoffman, Chicago, IL.

# Aunty Dare's Coffee Cake

Growing up, my favorite relative was great Aunt Claire, or "Aunty Dare," as I called her when I learned to talk. I spent hours and hours with her, from holidays to Friday night dinners and spent nearly my entire summer in her backyard. Even when I was young, I knew that we had a special bond—we just *got* each other. Plus, she was that "cool" aunt: When I was three years old, she had me over to watch *The Wizard of Oz,* because they actually had a color television.

Many of the memories I have of Aunt Claire are associated with food. Corned beef dipped in a special mixture of ketchup and mustard, eaten while lying on the kitchen floor; parsley new potatoes during Passover dinner; sweet-and-sour meatballs, heavy on the sauce; and, of course, her famous coffee cake.

When I turned sixteen, my parents threw a big sweet sixteen party for all of my relatives. Aware that I was Aunt Claire's favorite, everyone eagerly awaited what she might get me. When it came time to open her gift, she handed me a small note card wrapped in festive paper. It was her coffee cake recipe! I was thrilled and couldn't thank her enough, but the gift created quite the scandal amongst my relatives. "How could she just give her a recipe? What kind of aunt is she?" What no one knew was that she had also given me a beautiful set of luggage, which became our little secret.

Aunt Claire passed away a month after my sixteenth birthday, and the recipe immediately meant more to me than ever before. Today, it's my oldest recipe, and I bake the coffee cake whenever I'm with family. Even more than thirty years later, pulling out the recipe card puts a grin on my face and a warm hug in my heart.

**The Thoughts:**

Cake

½ c. margarine

¾ c. sugar

1 tsp. vanilla extract

3 eggs, room temperature

2 c. flour

1 tsp. baking soda

1 tsp. baking powder

1 c. sour cream

A sprinkling of connection

A teaspoon of understand

Crumble

6 Tbsp. margarine

1 c. brown sugar

2 tsp. cinnamon

1 c. pecans

A dash of "cool"

**Putting the Memory Together:**

Preheat oven to 350 degrees. For the cake, cream together margarine, sugar, and vanilla. Add eggs one at a time mixing after each addition. Sift flour, baking soda, and baking powder together. Add to sugar mixture alternately with the sour cream. To make the crumble, cream together the margarine, brown sugar, cinnamon, and pecans in a separate bowl. Grease a 10" tube pan and pour half of the batter into the pan. Sprinkle with half the crumble and repeat the layers one more time. Bake for fifty minutes. After eating, share recipe with the family member you love to spoil most!

Submitted by Elizabeth Pope, Hawthorn Woods, IL.

# Mom's Red Soup

My mom, Diane Christopherson, never said no to anyone. She was so giving, not a mean bone in her body. Whether it was a friend who needed a place to stay or a stray animal we found on the street, she never refused anyone. Everyone was welcome with open arms in our home. My dad used to say, "I pray to God no one drops an elephant in our front yard, because your mother will bring it in." When we were young, the number of people she'd invite over for dinner would gradually increase with every friend and neighbor that my three siblings and I added on. Eventually, there would be thirty or forty people in our house and our mom would be whipping up double batches of every dish. You could feel love just bursting at the seams. Known as "Mrs. C," she was one of the cool moms in the neighborhood. Supportive and non-judgmental, she made everyone feel better after talking to her.

My Mom had the hardest time saying no to her grandkids. Once we started having kids, she quit her job to take care of them, and loved every minute of it. But instead of bugging Grandma for candy or ice cream, they'd pester her to make her famous Red Soup. Though it was a simple tomato and beef soup, it was legendary in our family. It was my mother's grandmother's recipe, and a favorite of ours. She would make it for us whenever we were sick, and it was the best medicine—better than chicken soup—the best comfort food I have ever known.

Now, we all still crave Red Soup, and I'm thankful I was able to get the recipe. When I make it for my daughter, we always talk about Grandma. Though I do everything according to the recipe, my daughter always says, "You know, it's good. But it's still not as good as Grandma's." I guess it's just that special touch that grandparents have.

**The Thoughts:**

1 ½ to 2 lbs. pot roast
6 c. water
A dash of salt
1 bay leaf
10 whole black peppercorns
4 carrots, chopped
3 stalks of celery, chopped
1 small onion, chopped
1 (15 oz.) can diced tomatoes
1 or 2 cans tomato sauce
3 to 4 beef bouillon cubes
Noodles of your choice
A heaping spoonful of generosity
A cup of comfort
A handful of support
Sprinkle the magical touch of a grandparent, if you have it
(Note: Double the recipe in anticipation of extra guests)

**Putting the Memory Together:**

Bring water to boil. Send out a dinner invitation and watch it multiply. Add roast to water and boil for one and a half hours. Skim fat as necessary. Stir in remaining ingredients (except noodles) and cook for an hour or two. Add noodles and cook according to package directions. Serve to a loved one who needs a little comfort, whether it's physical or emotional. Offer a shoulder to cry on. Say yes.

Submitted by: Cathy Wildhurt, Woodridge, IL.

# Dad's Batter-First Brownies

On Sunday afternoon, our kitchen was the place to be,
As we sat at the counter waiting for Mom's specialty.
Anything chocolate would do for Dad,
But brownies were what we always had.
This deliciously chewy, chocolaty sweet
Was definitely Dad's favorite treat.
Around the Mixmaster we would gather,
Anxiously waiting to taste the batter.
A spoonful of sugar, a cup of flour,
We hoped they would be done before an hour.
The recipe was quick and easy,
But too much dough would make us queasy.
So into the oven they would go.
Dad could barely wait, he loved them so.
Undercooked was always his way;
We obviously had no say.
Once cool and ready to eat,
Dad finishing them was no small feat.
Making brownies was always a blast,
A memory that surely will last.
Made with love and laughter, as you can see,
A definite bittersweet memory.

## The Thoughts:

1 ⅓ c. all-purpose flour

¼ tsp. baking soda

¼ tsp. salt

1 ⅔ c. granulated sugar

½ c. butter or margarine, melted

4 oz. Nestle Toll House Choco Bake unsweetened chocolate flavoring

2 large eggs

2 Tbsp. water

1 ½ tsp. vanilla extract

A big ole' bowl

A handful of spoons

A sprinkle of laughter

## Putting the Memory Together:

Preheat oven to 350 degrees. Grease 13" x 9" baking pan. Combine flour, baking soda, and salt in small bowl and set aside. Stir sugar, butter, Choco Bake, eggs, water, and vanilla extract vigorously in large bowl. Stir in flour mixture. Grab a spoon and dig in, taking heaping spoonfuls of batter (Stop before feeling queasy!). Spread remaining batter into prepared baking pan. Bake for eighteen to twenty minutes, or less to keep them gooey and slightly undercooked. Best savored with laughter.

Submitted by Bari Anixter, Chicago, IL.

# Mom's Rugelach

When I was just beginning to date my future husband, he brought me over to his mother's house. Knowing she was sick, I told him I'd wait in the car to avoid inconveniencing someone who wasn't feeling well. Five minutes later, my boyfriend ran outside. His mom didn't want me sitting in the car and insisted that I come inside so she could meet me. I liked her right away.

Nineteen years after we were wed, my marriage to her son fell apart, but a lovely new friendship with my former mother-in-law, Saerree Fiedler, was just beginning. Unlike many families in a similar situation, she refused to let me go. As it turned out, we had more in common as single ladies, a widow and a divorcée. We'd meet for coffee or dinner, or I'd head over to her house for conversations over freshly baked goods. Several years after the divorce, we both became involved with new companions. The four of us would double date, and our new gentlemen became good friends.

She was a good cook, and while her home was always full of the smells and tastes of baked treats, it was rugelach that the family craved—so much so that when Saerree would make a batch, relatives would take to hoarding them. Siblings hid them from each other, parents tucked them away from their kids (the hiding spots remain completely confidential). When I first married her son, Saerree pulled me into the kitchen to make it with her, passing along a family treasure. This year, I'll do the same with my own daughter, keeping Saerree's generous, loving spirit alive. Whoever said anything negative about mothers-in-law never met mine!

## The Thoughts:

3 eggs, beaten
½ lb. melted butter
8 oz. sour cream
½ c. sugar
4 c. flour
1 or 2 packages dry yeast
A sprinkling of friendship
A shake of unconditional love

Topping:

3 Tbsp. Melted butter
⅓ c. Sugar
2 tsp. Cinnamon
1 c. Nuts
¾ c. Raisins
Connection
Good conversation

## Putting the Memory Together:

Before baking, invite someone special into the kitchen to bake with you. Connect over conversation. Combine eggs and butter. Add sour cream and mix together. Add sugar, flour, and yeast. Place in refrigerator overnight. Remove and allow to return to room temperature for about thirty minutes. Cut into four sections. Roll out each section as you would a piecrust (about one-eighth inches thick) and sprinkle with topping ingredients. Cut into narrow wedges (about one to one and a half inches wide) and roll up. Let stand for thirty minutes. Bake at 350 degrees for twenty to twenty-five minutes on greased cookie sheet. Remove from oven and, when no one is looking, stash a few pieces to ensure it doesn't disappear too quickly. When the rugelach is all gone, whip out the secret stash and share with a loved one.

Submitted by Dottie Fiedler, Deerfield, IL.

# Mantecaditos (Shortbread Cookies)

I lived in Puerto Rico until I was twenty-four. We lived about an hour or so from my grandparents, and I loved to visit them. My grandmother was from Sevilla, Spain, and their home was always cheerfully bursting with sevillanas and flamenco music. Beautiful paintings hung all over their walls. But the best part was that their home was always packed with goodies. Neapolitan ice cream? Of course. Hershey's kisses? You got it. Homemade lasagna, lemon bars, mantecaditos? Always available. Their home was a twenty-four hour food haven. My grandmother always had enough food to feed an army of people, from the most exquisite appetizers to at least four different entrees. We would all sit at the big table to hear them talk about the "good old times" and listen to music. After lunch, we would flip through the pages of their old photo albums while sipping coffee, Cointreau, or Anis del Mono. It was always the same routine and I loved every part of it.

Later, I moved to Chicago, but when my children were born, I brought them down to meet their great-grandparents. My grandfather couldn't get enough of my daughter. Even though everyone knows Lucia is my husband's little clone, he kept saying, "Oh, Nina! She looks just like you!" When he held Joaquin he would gush, "He is going to be a movie star, Nina! What a beautiful little boy!" Though there wasn't any homemade cooking then, the energy in my grandparents' condo was as cheerful as ever, and we spent an unforgettable day with them. That was the last time I saw my grandfather. Though they may not remember it, I'm grateful that my children got to meet my grandparents and, more importantly, that my grandparents got to meet them.

**The Thoughts:**

2 ¼ c. all-purpose flour

¼ tsp. ground nutmeg

¾ c. butter

¼ c. vegetable shortening

1 ¼ tsp. almond extract

½ tsp. vanilla extract

½ c. granulated sugar

¼ c. confectioners sugar (optional)

A dash of cheer

A heaping teaspoon of joy

A sprinkle of nostalgia

**Putting the Memory Together:**

Put on your family's favorite music. Preheat oven to 350 degrees. Combine flour and nutmeg in a bowl and set aside. In a large bowl, beat butter, vegetable shortening, vanilla extract, and almond extract until very smooth. Cream in sugar until smooth. Gradually blend in the flour mixture. It should be light and not sticky. Shape teaspoons of dough into little balls. Place on ungreased cookie sheet and bake for eighteen minutes, or until golden brown. Cool on a wire rack and sprinkle with powdered sugar. Serve with an array of other irresistible goodies, and bring out the photo albums.

Submitted by: Nina Goyco, Fishers, IN.

# There's Nothing Like Sour Cream Noodle Bake

My mother, Kay, loved to cook and was always looking for new recipes to try. When I was young, she would watch Graham Kerr, "The Galloping Gourmet," on television and write down the recipes on a yellow legal pad—a habit she'd picked up as a secretary. As we got older, we all looked forward to dinners at my mother's house. They were *events*, whether it was a Thanksgiving dinner for twenty, a feast for our visiting Irish relatives, or a meal for one of us kids home from college. She was a great cook, and she would always create a gourmet meal that everyone eagerly anticipated.

I spent my life as a career Army Officer, serving two stints in Korea and two stints in Iraq (Desert Shield and Desert Storm). My wife and kids lived near my parents and relied heavily on their help while I was away. When I would come home, it was always an enormous and special occasion. All the relatives would come over. As soon as I walked in the door, my mom would ask, "What do you want?" She was an incredibly talented chef, and there were hundreds of dishes she could have whipped up for me. But I would always respond, "sour cream noodle bake."

My mother never understood why, when she could make superb shrimp scampi or delicious veal Francese, I would want something as simple as sour cream noodle bake. What she never understood was that I had been around the world and had enjoyed myriad delicacies, from steak tartare in Paris to yachae mandu in Korea, but nothing I found ever said home like sour cream noodle bake. It was something that no one else made and the one thing that, no matter where I was, I could never find. Some approximation of her other simple, home-cooked dishes might be found in the Army mess halls, but I never, ever found anything that even came close to sour cream noodle bake.

My parents both died in 2002, within nine months of each other. Though my parents did well and owned a beautiful house on the Jersey Shore, my brother and sisters didn't argue a bit over the division of their estate or the disposition of their possessions. The only thing we all wanted was the recipe for sour cream noodle bake, written in my mother's own hand, on a piece of yellow legal paper.

**The Thoughts:**

12 oz. egg noodles

1 lb. ground beef

1 small onion

1 tsp. garlic powder

1 tsp. each salt and pepper

16 oz. tomato sauce

8 oz. sour cream

8 oz. cottage cheese

8 oz. extra sharp cheddar cheese

A big, welcoming greeting

A heaping tablespoon of home

**Putting the Memory Together:**

Preheat oven to 350 degrees. Cook egg noodles according to package directions and set aside. Brown the meat and onions with salt, pepper, and garlic powder. Drain excess oil. Add in tomato sauce and simmer. Mix sour cream and cottage cheese with the cooked egg noodles in a deep casserole dish. Pour meat and sauce mixture on top. Sprinkle with cheddar cheese. Bake for forty-five to sixty minutes, or until hot in the center. Savor alongside the other comforts of home, sweet home.

Submitted by Joseph O'Donnell, Yorktown, VA.

# Meat, Rice, and Peas

My youngest son, Sergeant Clint William Dickey, was the kind of kid you wanted to be around. He was fun, charismatic, lively, smart, and naturally athletic. When he was fourteen, a friend from church convinced him to run a 5K. He was usually up for anything, and when he got home, he was carrying a three foot trophy.

"Clint!" I asked, surprised. "What happened?"

"Well, I got second place in the under nineteen group."

"Congratulations!" I said, shocked.

"Yeah, well, I would have been faster if I hadn't stopped at the Jack in the Box to go to the bathroom!" He told me matter-of-factly.

Clint joined the Army Reserves to pay for his tuition to Texas A&M. He was proud to protect his country. He served in Afghanistan for two tours as a member of the 345 Airborne Unit. He came home safely, save for two slipped discs in his back that caused him a great deal of pain. But soon after his return, he was diagnosed with post-traumatic stress disorder. On February 13, 2010, just over a month after he had married his college sweetheart, Samantha Serene Dickey, he died. The official cause of death was accidental overdose: He had a panic attack as a result of PTSD and accidentally took too much of his back medication.

They held a full military funeral for my son. The attendees included his past teammates, friends, and fellow soldiers. After the burial, his superiors handed me a traditionally folded flag and the shell casings from the twenty-one gun salute. His funeral was on the front page of the Waco newspaper, and soon after, they wrote a large story on Clint and the epidemic of soldiers with PTSD. I believe this was Clint's mission. I trust in God's plan, and I believe that Clint was meant to raise public awareness of PTSD.

This recipe is simple, but it was Clint's favorite. He would come home from Texas A&M with Samantha and his friends and I'd put a big ole' bowl of meat, rice, and peas on the table, and they would scarf it down like there was no tomorrow.

**The Thoughts:**

1 lb. lean ground beef

1 pkg. chicken flavor Rice-A-Roni (or equivalent)

1 can English peas

A blend of courage and honor

A sprinkling of tragedy

A heaping handful of trust

**Putting the Memory Together:**

Brown ground beef in a skillet and drain. Set aside. Cook rice mix per package directions and add beef, seasoning mix, and water. Simmer rice mixture accordingly, adding peas five minutes before the rice is done. Place in a large bowl in front of hungry, homesick college kids with several forks and spoons and watch it disappear.

Submitted by Beverley Dickey, Waco, TX.

# Grandpa Jack's Breakfast

My Grandpa Jack was the greatest person I ever knew. He taught me how to hunt and fish and showed me everything I needed to know about working in a woodshop. But, before we could start our days together, he'd fry up breakfast, and we'd feed half of the bacon to his Pomeranian dog, Pepper. Oh, how he hated doing the dishes after breakfast. As soon as we had finished, he'd always say, "Now the damned dishes!"

Grandpa Jack passed away in his sleep on March 1, 2010. Something happened the day he died, something that you don't really understand unless it has happened to you. He came to me in a dream. I saw him on the street by my house, restored to health and dressed in his best striped shirt and Wrangler jeans. In my vision, I ran out to meet him. I remember it being so beautiful outside and I asked him, "Grandpa, where are you going?" He smiled down at me, then looked up and said softly, "Home. I'm going home." I asked, "Home? You mean back up to the mountains?" He replied, "No, Jonathan, I'm going home." Then he turned and walked into this blinding, beautiful white light and disappeared. I woke up immediately and was confused—I had never really seen such a thing in my life. I didn't understand it until thirty minutes later, when I found out that he had passed away while sleeping. It all made sense. He wanted me to see him go, to give me the last of his love. He meant a great deal to me, and I meant a great deal to him. I sure do miss him, especially at breakfast.

**The Thoughts:**

2 eggs
4 slices of bacon or sausage links (or both)
2 pieces of toast
A dash of love
A heaping spoonful of adventure
A slab of companionship

**Putting the Memory Together:**

Fry up ingredients for a loved one. Enjoy with orange juice and morning conversation. Upon completion, say together, "Now the damned dishes!"

Submitted by Jon Gies, Lewistown, MT.

# Santa Lucia Polenta

Two giant pots simmered on the stove, both so large they each required two burners. My grandmother stirred the cornmeal mixture with a wooden spoon, maintaining a watchful eye while the polenta thickened. Bubbling next to the cornmeal was the "gravy," a rich tomato sauce seasoned with basil that had been cooking all day. A giant hardwood cutting board covered the entire kitchen table. On this night, we didn't have to set the table, bare wood was all we needed.

It was December 13, the feast of Santa Lucia, or St. Lucy, the patron saint of Sicily. On this day each year, dinner was literally served on the kitchen table.

"*Venire qui*," my grandmother called. "It's ready." We all grabbed a spoon from the drawer and raced to the table. The pan was so heavy that it took both my mother and grandmother to lift it, pouring the polenta in the center of the table. We watched as yellow mounds rolled across the board. Next, a sea of deep red sauce flowed through the center. Streams of the tomato gravy rippled out to the edges, eventually reaching our spoons.

"Move, this is my section," I said, pushing my brother's spoon away from my elbow. "*Ferma te*! There's room for everyone," my mother scolded. There were more than ten of us around the table—cousins, aunts, uncles, my siblings—all waiting to scoop our first bite, all worried that we wouldn't get a large enough section. We claimed our area and began to eat. The room would go silent as we savored our first mouthfuls, but soon the dinner table conversation took on its usual lively tone. We gobbled our own sections and then moved our bites toward the middle. It always surprised me how, at the end of meal, even with ten or more people around the table, there was always polenta left on the board.

**The Thoughts:**

Sauce:

¼ c. olive oil
½ c. chopped onion
2 cloves garlic, minced
⅛ tsp. red pepper flakes
⅛ tsp. fresh chopped basil
3 ½ c. whole tomatoes, sieved
3 ½ c. tomato puree
¼ tsp fresh parsley, chopped
1 tsp. salt
A dash of festivity
A friendly dash of competition

Polenta:

5 c. water
1 tsp. salt
1 ½ c. cornmeal
½ c. parmesan cheese
Extra cheese for top
A large table
Many, many spoons

**Putting the Memory Together:**

Sauce:

Place oil in pan. Add onion, garlic, red pepper, and basil. Sauté three minutes over medium heat. Add tomatoes, tomato puree, parsley, and salt. Bring to boil. Lower heat and simmer for forty-five minutes. If you wish to simmer longer, add additional liquid (water or tomato puree) as necessary.

Polenta:

Put water and salt in large saucepan. Slowly add cornmeal, stirring constantly with large metal whisk. Bring to boil. Stir in parmesan cheese. Cover and let simmer forty-five minutes to one hour. Stir every ten minutes. When ready, grab an assistant for help and pour polenta onto large board, plate, or table. Top with sauce. Sprinkle additional cheese on top. Place dozens of spoons around the polenta and let the family loose. Be on the lookout for polenta competition, and counter with a friendly reminder that there's enough to go around. (Note: If you have any leftover polenta, its great fried in a pan for breakfast!)

Submitted by Mary Joe Guglielmo, Chicago, IL.

# Gramma's Molasses Sugar Cookies

My grandmother, Carmen, was the perfect dairy farmer's wife. She was Norwegian and all about hospitality. Whenever you walked into her house, the first thing she would say was, "Are you hungry?" She wasn't the best cook in the world, but she was a fantastic baker and always had some kind of freshly baked goodies ready to devour. Everyone loved her food, but a particular favorite was her molasses sugar cookies.

I was fortunate to grow up next door to my grandparents in rural Wisconsin. My grandfather had a huge dairy farm, and my parents had twelve acres about a quarter of a mile away. A small dirt lane connected the two homes. My grandfather's cows would walk down the lane to their favorite grazing area in the woods. I would take that lane to Grandma and Grandpa's house whenever I was bored. When Maria, my best friend, and I would play together, we usually ended up traveling down to see what treats my grandma had made that day. She never disappointed—after indulging in cookies and fresh milk from my grandpa's milk house, she always sent us back to my house with a baggie of cookies for later.

There wasn't any daycare where I lived, so while my parents worked, I would spend the day with my grandma at their small farmhouse. As we baked together in the kitchen, she would teach me about my Norwegian heritage, cooking the foods and sharing the language. She would often show me the dances that she used to do with her friends at dance halls before she met my grandfather.

Grandmas are a special breed. Now, being one myself, I try to do with my own grandchildren the things that she did with me. I wonder what my grandkids will look back on as the defining moments of me as a grandmother—the same way I remember my grandma dancing while cooking, teaching me to speak Norwegian, and savoring cookies and milk with me in the kitchen?

## The Thoughts:

¾ c. shortening

1 c. sugar

¼ c. molasses (dark molasses preferred)

1 egg

2 c. flour

2 tsp. baking soda

½ tsp. cloves

½ tsp. ginger

1 tsp. cinnamon

½ tsp. salt

A blend of quality time

A dose of heritage

A heaping teaspoon of legacy

## Putting the Memory Together:

First, ask "Are you hungry?" Regardless of the answer, begin to bake. Mix all ingredients together well. Chill. (Grandma's note: "I just let them sit awhile. The sugar sticks better.") Form into 1" inch balls and roll in additional granulated sugar. Place two inches apart on a cookie sheet. Bake in oven at 350 degrees for ten minutes. (Grandma's note: "I never time them. You have to watch them real closely after they start to crack. They burn easily.") Best served with singing and dancing with languages and memories.

Submitted by Dana Goheen, Glen Ellyn, IL.

# Grandma Mark's Apple Cake

When the air started to smell crisp and the leaves began to change, my family would always take a trip to Tanner's Apple Orchard. It was an extended family excursion, and my mom, aunts, cousins and Grandma Laverne would walk up and down the rows of trees and pick apples. When we came home, Grandma Laverne would bake my family's favorite apple cake. The recipe originated from my grandfather's mother, Grandma Mark, but I can only remember my Grandma Laverne making this delicious cake, which made the house smell like fall. She would spread dozens of apples out on the dining room table and peel them by hand. She was very sentimental and would never think of using a more modern apple-peeling contraption. I used to love sitting and helping at the dining room table.

Every Sunday night, she and my grandfather hosted a huge meal. Grandma Laverne always cooked for at least twelve people, even when only four were there. She always brought leftovers to those who couldn't make it. Their home was a revolving door and their kitchen was always full of delicious sweets, pies, cobblers and, of course, delicious apple cake.

Grandma and I continued our baking tradition as I grew up. She and my grandfather eventually moved into my parents' home, and I would make the three-hour drive from Chicago to Peoria to spend time with them. Baking together, my grandma and I never missed a chance to reminisce about the way things used to be.

## The Thoughts:

2 c. sugar

1 c. canola oil

1 tsp. vanilla

2 eggs, beaten

4 c. finely chopped apples

2 c. flour

2 tsp. cinnamon

1 tsp. salt

1 tsp. baking soda

A dollop of family tradition

## Putting the Memory Together:

Spread freshly picked apples out on a large table and surround with loving family. Peel and chop apples, old-fashioned style, while exchanging stories. Preheat oven to 325 degrees. Blend sugar, oil, vanilla, eggs, and apples. Add flour, cinnamon, salt, and baking soda. Batter will be stiff. Spread batter into a greased 13" x 9" cake pan. Bake for one to one and a half hours. Serve warm with vanilla bean ice cream. For an extra grandma's touch, soften a quart of vanilla bean ice cream, blend in 1 tsp. of cinnamon, and refreeze until serving. Finally, fold in the sights and smells of autumn and garnish with a dose of nostalgia.

Submitted by Stephanie Hlinak, Chicago, IL.

# Magic Cookie Bars

My mom, Bonnie, passed away from melanoma when I was eight years old. Because I was so young, I only have a few memories of her. She was a brilliant piano player, an excellent teacher, a loving young mother of three, and a great cook. A few years ago, I rediscovered her blue, tattered recipe box in a cluttered closet in my childhood home. Though I'd known it was there for some time, finding it again resonated much more clearly: now I am also a mother of three. Since I was at her age that I remembered her most clearly, she suddenly became alive to me.

Looking through her recipes, I was delighted to see her beautiful handwriting scrawled across three by five inch index cards, on the backs of church service programs, on scraps of paper or paper towels, and on *Family Circle* clippings. Reading through the box was like discovering pieces of her that I never knew. Recipes like "Snickerdoodles from Sandy" tell of a social circle that loved sharing recipes. Directions for "Same-Day Sauerbraten" point to an adventurous palate. A recipe for toffee with a note that says, "Make only on pay day" hints at her sense of humor. And five identical recipes for "Magic Cookie Bars"—three handwritten and two ripped form the back of condensed milk cans—reveal what I'm certain must have been one of her favorite treats.

In making these recipes for my family, I am struck with a powerful feeling of longing for my mother. But I am also overcome with a sense of calm and connection and a true feeling of peace.

## The Thoughts:

½ c. butter or margarine

1 ½ c. graham cracker crumbs

½ c. chopped nuts

1 c. chocolate chips

1 ⅓ c. flaked coconut

1 can (14 oz.) sweetened condensed milk

A heaping spoonful of sentimentality

A dollop of longing

## Putting the Memory Together:

Melt butter in 13" x 9" pan. Sprinkle graham cracker crumbs evenly over butter. Sprinkle on nuts, chocolate chips, and coconut. Pour condensed milk evenly over mixture. Bake at 350 degrees for twenty-five minutes or until lightly browned on top. Cool in pan fifteen minutes. Cut into bars. Take the first bite while savoring the handwriting of a lost loved one. Look for clues about their life as you are transported through a world of memory.

Submitted by: Lisa Mahoney, Arlington, MA.

# Grandma Rose's Plum Chicken with Rice and Bean Casserole

I got my first real grandma when I was twenty-five years old. I had been dating my husband for about six months when we ventured to Florida to meet his Grandma Rose. I wasn't close to my own grandmothers, so I had never understood the grandmother/granddaughter relationship. After meeting Grandma Rose, I finally understood what it was all about. Small in stature but with an oversized personality, Rose filled a room with her dynamic energy. She was nurturing and motherly with a solution for everything. Every time I left her to return home, she'd give me a pile of books that looked innocent enough but quickly revealed themselves as the trashiest, smuttiest, make-you-blush romance novels I've ever read. That's Rose in a nutshell. We were great friends.

The most important thing I learned from Grandma Rose was how to cook. Every year, we'd travel down to Florida and stay with her, and every morning she would ask us what we wanted for breakfast, lunch, and dinner. She cooked every meal. We didn't want her to go through all the trouble, but she could not be deterred. For Grandma Rose, food was love, and she was showing us how much she cared.

I used to ask her for recipes for her delicious dishes—drunken chicken with scotch, lox and eggs—and she'd give them to me happily. But at home, when I cooked her food, it never tasted quite the same. "Rose, mine doesn't taste like yours. What did I do wrong?" I'd ask over the phone. She would respond, "Well, did you add the ____?" Of course, it was an ingredient that she had neglected to share. I would reply, "Rose, are you holding out on me again?" She would laugh. It was the same every time. She would always withhold the top-secret ingredient that made the dish authentically Rose. I wised up after a few years and followed her around the kitchen with a pen and paper. While they still don't taste exactly the same, they still evoke the unique image of Grandma Rose.

## The Thoughts:

Plum Chicken

¼ tsp. pepper

1 jar (12 oz.) plum jelly

⅓ c. brown sugar

⅓ c. soy sauce

2 Tbsp. lemon juice

⅓ c. dry sherry

1 onion, sliced

2 chickens, cut in parts

1 tsp. garlic salt

A dash of surprise

A dollop of kitchen education

A pen and paper

## Putting the Memory Together:

Combine pepper, plum jelly, brown sugar, soy sauce, lemon juice, and dry sherry and bring to a boil. Remove from heat. Scatter sliced onions across the bottom of a 13" x 9" pan. Season chicken with garlic salt and set atop onions. Make sure you haven't forgotten any important ingredients, and if you have, hassle the recipe holder until the information is revealed. Pour the plum jelly mixture over chicken and bake at 350 degrees for one hour and forty-five minutes. Baste chicken frequently. Best served with rice and bean casserole.

Rice and Bean Casserole

16 oz. package fresh sliced mushrooms
1 large onion
½ c. butter
1 can (15 oz.) black beans

2 c. chicken broth

**Putting the Memory Together:**

Dice mushrooms and onions. Sauté onions in butter until sweating and opaque. Add mushrooms and continue to sauté until onions are brown and mushrooms are cooked through. Set aside.

Prepare rice according to package, using chicken broth in place of water. Rinse and drain black beans. When rice is finished, add black beans and onion mixture. Mix together in oven-safe dish and let sit at room temperature. Heat in the oven for thirty minutes while the chicken finishes cooking.

Submitted by: Leslie Kolber, Northbrook, IL.

# Simple (but Delicious) Brisket

When my sons, Leif and Jared, were growing up, I cooked every night. We sat at the table together—cloth napkins and tablecloths included—and chatted about the day. We lived in Miller Beach in Gary, Indiana, where there wasn't much to do, so many of our weekends included potluck dinners with all of our friends and their children. We created our own family, and food was a big part of our lives.

We were a diverse group, so our children got to celebrate all of the holidays. I hosted the Jewish occasions, serving up brisket and matzo ball soup in our small dining room. On holidays, it often swelled with more than twenty people.

Around my fiftieth birthday, I needed major surgery. Both of my sons came home from school for the weekend. Leif and his then-girlfriend had the idea to make a typical Jewish holiday meal—if only I would give the instructions. It was truly the most memorable meal of my life. I sat on a chair in the living room and said, "You do this. Now do that. And you, do this!" It was all done close to perfection, right down to the setting of the table. The boys invited many of their friends to this home-cooked feast, and that night, they told me horror stories of the mischief they'd gotten into when they were younger— how they and their friends used to come and go at all hours of the night through the basement door. I hadn't a clue about any of it.

In 2008, Leif died in a car accident. I miss him every minute of every day, but this brisket recipe always connects me to his memory.

## The Thoughts:

4 lb. brisket, trimmed of excess fat

24 oz. beef bouillon

3 large onions

1 lb. carrots

3 lb. small red potatoes (skins on)

A dollop of direction

A pinch of generosity

A diverse blend of friends and family

## Putting the Memory Together:

Preheat oven to 350 degrees. Slice onions and lay out on the bottom of a large roasting pan. Place brisket on top. Pour bouillon over brisket and cook for three to four hours. Let cool and refrigerate entire pot overnight.

The next day, slice the cold brisket and return to roasting pan with bouillon and onions. Place potatoes and carrots atop brisket. Cook at 350 degrees for two to three hours until the potatoes are soft and the carrots are nicely steamed. Separate potatoes and carrots and serve as side dishes. Potatoes can be served mashed or as is and carrots can be served with a little parsley. Best eaten with a blend of friends and family and garnished with a sprig of mischievous secrets revealed.

Submitted by Karen Lieberman, Hollywood, FL.

# Mom's Perfect Pie Crust

Although my mother was always a wonderful cook and baker, she never had confidence in her abilities—perhaps because she came from a family of incredible cooks. Her mother was renowned for her culinary talent. My mom, for her part, didn't learn to cook until after she was married.

When my mother was a newlywed, she and my father moved to rural Canada, where my father did a general practice stint in Saskatchewan after his residency. When my mother spoke about this time in her life, she described it as being stranded in the country, knowing no one, and learning to cook for my father. One day, she tried to make a pie. When my father left for work in the morning, she was rolling out her pie crust. By the time he returned at lunch, my mom was in the exact same place, rolling out the same pie crust, now in tears. My mom was nearly inconsolable, so my dad ended up finishing the crust. It came out tough as leather, of course!

Though she got much, much better in the kitchen—and her pie crust was eventually perfected—that insecurity remained. No matter what my mother made, whether it was a brand-new recipe or a one-hundredth batch, she would ask if it was okay. If you said something like, "It's delicious," she would pretend not to hear and ask, "What?" She just wanted to hear the validation again. It became a family joke. We would always be ready to tell my mom that a dish was delicious twice. Today, I find myself repeating this behavior with my own family, asking "What?" when they compliment our dinners, a smile on my face as I pass on her legacy in more ways than one.

## The Thoughts:

3 c. all-purpose flour

1 tsp. salt

½ c. very cold butter, cubed

½ c. very cold shortening, cubed

1 egg

2 tsp. vinegar

2 tsp. lemon juice

Ice water

1 Tbsp. vanilla sugar or white sugar

## Putting the Memory Together:

In a food processor fitted with a metal blade (can also be done by hand), blend flour with salt. Pulse in butter and shortening until mixture resembles fine crumbs with a few larger pieces. In a 1 cup measuring cup, beat egg until foamy. Add vinegar, lemon juice, sugar, and enough ice water to make two thirds of a cup. With food processor running, add egg mixture all at once to dough mixture. Process until dough just starts to clump together. Do not let it form a ball. Remove and press together into two equal disks. Wrap disks in plastic wrap and chill for at least thirty minutes or up to three days. Let cold pastry stand for fifteen minutes at room temperature before rolling out. When ready, place a large piece of waxed paper on top of each dough disk and roll outwards, starting from the center of the disk, until you have reached preferred thinness. Makes two single nine or ten inch pie crusts.

Submitted by: Enid Barnes, Shorewood, WI.

# Snowy Day Baked Apples

Growing up north of Chicago, long, snowy, and frigid winters have always been a part of my life and my weekday routine. At 3:15 p.m., the school bus would drop me off at the end of my street and I would tiredly trudge home through the snowdrifts as the winter wind whipped at my cheeks. After a long day at school, all I wanted to do was go home, curl up, and happily watch the quiet snowflakes from inside my warm house.

When I walked through the front door, the smell of apples and cinnamon would instantly erase any troubles I had: a bad grade, a fight with a friend, snow tucked inside my boots. I'd make a beeline for the kitchen where my mom would be sitting on a stool, dressed in her comfortable snowy day clothes, waiting for me with a gorgeous platter of red baked apples on the table. She would pour thick Coffee Rich creamer over the apples and ask me about my day as I dug into the sweet, warm fruit.

Whenever I smell an apple pie or see baked apples on a menu, I'm taken back to those cold winter days when I sat snugly in our kitchen, snow falling gently outside and my mom making me feel warm and safe inside.

**The Thoughts:**

4 large baking apples, such as Rome Beauty, Golden Delicious, or Jonagold

¼ c. brown sugar

1 tsp. cinnamon

1 Tbsp. butter

¾ cup boiling water

**Putting the Memory Together:**

Preheat oven to 375 degrees. Wash apples. Remove cores, leaving a half inch at the bottom of the apples. It helps if you have an apple corer. If not, use a paring knife to cut out the stem area and the core, and then use a spoon to dig out the seeds. Make the holes three quarters of an inch to one inch wide.

In a small bowl, combine sugar and cinnamon. Place apples in an 8" x 8" square baking pan. Stuff each apple with sugar mixture and top with ¼ Tbsp. of butter. Add boiling water to the baking pan. Bake for thirty to forty minutes until tender but not mushy. Remove from oven and baste apples several times with pan juices. Serve warm with vanilla ice cream (or Coffee Rich creamer) on the side. Makes 4 servings.

Submitted By: Emily Israel Hoffman, Chicago, IL.

# Chapter 3

## Healing through Laughter Intro

**"Remember, men need laughter sometimes more than food."**
**— Anna Fellows Johnston**

My mom had this wonderfully distinct laugh. When something was funny, so funny that she couldn't catch her breath, her laugh would get caught in the back of her throat. She would make this "ooh-ooh-ooh" sound, like a monkey, which only made everyone around her laugh that much harder. She would always finish with a huge sigh of relief and say, "There's nothing like a good laugh."

My mother's humorous mantra is one that I occasionally cling to for dear life when I'm stressed out by the daily grind or overwhelmed with missing her. The image of my mother clutching her chest, her head thrown back in pure joy, her face radiating as she "ooh-ooh-oohs," has an instantly soothing effect. I can't help but smile. My pulse slows down, my mind stops reeling, and, sometimes for the first time that day, week, month, I can stop and relish the wave of calm and joy that washes over me. The best part? As the image of my mother laughing plays through my mind, it snowballs, summoning a slideshow of my family's funniest moments: the time my uncle Harry brought a farting machine to a holiday dinner, or when my dad accidentally chugged a Mike's Hard Lemonade (thinking it was a real lemonade) after a run, every single time my mom somehow ruined beef brisket, or even just sitting on my mom's bed with my sisters, aunts, and cousins talking and laughing. Remembering not just the happy moments but also the hilarious ones has a way of lifting my spirits and carrying me through difficult spots until I feel like I can function again.

Allowing yourself to smile and laugh is essential to the healing process. Even when grief has you pinned down like a champion wrestler, just a small smile (even if it's forced at first) has a way of traveling through your mind and body until you're actually feeling happy. Sometimes, it's not that easy. "When a loved one passes away, you want to hold on to that person, and mourning is, in essence, a way to hold on to them," says psychologist Mary Beth Paul. "In those first few months, when you laugh, you almost pull it back. You think that when you start to feel good again, you will lose the connection to him or her."

To be completely honest, there are some days when it feels kind of good to wallow in your sadness, curl up in bed with a cozy blanket and a bowlful of memories. But there's a fine line between wallowing and drowning. I:n order to stay afloat, you need to cling to every rope of happiness, letting even the smallest smile to lift you up. "Even though it feels like your world stops and that you're lost in grief, when something makes you laugh—despite the mourning, despite the sadness—the very fact that you're laughing means you are still alive," says Paul.

The effects of laughter on our entire system have been well documented. As it turns out, laughing is essential to maintaining our health and happiness. Decades of research suggests that laughter boosts our immune system, promotes a healthy diaphragm and lung capacity, lowers our blood pressure, increases organ health (by increasing blood flow), and oxygenates the blood, which gives us a healthy glow and increases energy. Most importantly, a good laugh releases endorphins—the "feel good" neurotransmitter—in the brain, lifting spirits even after they've been low for far too long. The effects of a good laugh can last for nearly forty-five minutes. After you've lost someone you love, even forty-five minutes of feeling good is a blessing.

After losing my mother, surrounding myself with people who made me laugh made all the difference. That's where my husband came in. D.J. and I met ten months before my mother passed away. Needless to say, we were going through some particularly hard times when most couples are savoring their honeymoon phase. But D.J. has this amazing way of lifting my spirits, even when I'm at my lowest. He's one of the funniest people I have ever met, and he always had the perfect quip or comment that would make me burst out laughing—even while tears were streaming down my face. In those first few anguish-filled months after losing my mom, D.J. and I laughing together would take away the seriousness and intensity of our lives. Just for a small moment, we would have only the pleasure of being together. Though we began our life together on a rough and rocky road, we navigated it side by side, with D.J.'s humor the map to a clearer path.

Healing is a lifelong process. It's like cutting your hand while slicing vegetables.. At first, it's raw, tender, and glaringly obvious. But eventually, life starts to happen again. It takes your mind off the cut, distracts you and demands your attention. Suddenly, you can see clearly again. Over time, a scab begins to form, and the injury becomes less noticeable—though you will see and feel the scar every day for the rest of your life. Even during the most excruciating moments, when you think you'll never feel joy again, every smile and every laugh is a healing salve that brings you one step closer to happiness.

# Mom's "Welcome to the Family" Kugel

My mother had just hired a new housekeeper, Tatiana. On her first day, my mother asked Tatiana to join us for dinner. We were eating one of my mom's "go-to" meals: salad, chicken, and kugel. Kugel, a traditional Jewish dish, is a sweet noodle casserole that resembles a Jewish lasagna.

Tatiana did not say much that night. At the time, she had difficulty speaking English and sat very quietly at the table as she ate her dinner.

The television happened to be on in the kitchen that night. My mother must have forgotten to turn it off, so the nightly news played on even though none of us paid attention.

After we had all finished our meal, we sat around the table talking. After about ten minutes, my father went into the family room to watch television more comfortably. Our TV was hooked up to a satellite system, so the channel could be changed and viewed from any room in the house. As my father started clicking through, it was clear he had forgotten that the TV was on in the kitchen. Suddenly, Tatiana's eyes got huge, and her face turned as red as a tomato. My mother looked around to see what had happened, and that's when she saw it: the Playboy Channel, blaring from the television.

She yelled to my father to change to channel immediately. We were all incredibly embarrassed, but we laughed about it all night. I still laugh when I imagine what must have been going through Tatiana's head. She stayed with our family for many years, but on that first night, she must have wondered what she had gotten herself into. Needless to say, from that point on, the television was always turned off during dinnertime.

**The Thoughts:**

1 lb. No Yolk extra-wide egg noodles

16 oz. small-curd cottage cheese

16 oz. sour cream

1 c. sugar

4 eggs

¾ c. margarine

A pinch of salt

A dash of surprise

A heaping spoonful of laughter

Topping:

1 ½ c. Cornflake Crumbs

2 tsp. Cinnamon

3 Tbsp. Margarine

**Putting the Memory Together:**

Invite all family members—immediate, extended, and adopted—over to dine. Cook noodles according to package directions and drain. Mix in remaining ingredients (not including topping) and put in 8" x 11" glass dish. Sprinkle cornflake crumbs and cinnamon over top and then dot with margarine. Bake, uncovered, at 350 degrees for one hour. Turn off all televisions before eating, savor good conversations, and share hilarious family memories

Submitted by: Emily Israel Hoffman, Chicago, IL

# Bonnie's Pie-in-the-Face Banana Cream Pie

To know my dad, Dave, was a privilege, but I always slept with one eye open: he was a jokester. One of my favorite memories of him includes the banana cream pie my mother, Bonnie, proudly made for the first time.

While Bonnie was a wonderful cook, effortlessly whipping up dishes like brisket, clam linguini, and pizza from scratch, she seldom baked. But one day, she spent all day in the kitchen, slaving over her first-ever banana cream pie. After our delicious dinner, my mom brought the pie out of the refrigerator and placed it gingerly on the table. My dad smiled at her and told her how good it looked. He picked the whole pie up, admiring its peaks of whip cream and perfectly browned crust and complimenting my mother's baking abilities. Then, he put his nose close to the pie and smelled it.

"Bonnie, I think it smells funny," he said. "Did you use fresh ingredients?" He looked over at my brother and me with a twinkle in his eye.

"Of course I did," she said. With a confused look, she leaned down and put her nose close to the pie's whip cream topping. That's when chaos broke loose. As she inhaled, my dad lifted his hand and pushed the pie right into her face. As my mom stood there, stunned, wearing an *I'm going to kill you* look beneath gobs of banana filling and whipped cream, my brother reached into the remainder of the pie, pulled out a chunk and threw it right at me. I retaliated, and in seconds, my dad, brother, and I were in an all-out banana cream pie fight, decorating each other and our kitchen walls with the remnants of my mom's first baked good.

"I just couldn't pass up the opportunity," my dad said, laughing, his eyes sparkling. We licked the remains off our hands, and lo and behold, the pie was delicious.

**The Thoughts:**

Crust:

⅓ c. melted butter

1 ¼ c. graham cracker crumbs

2 Tbsp. sugar

A dash of surprise

A dose of humor

Filling:

⅔ c. sugar

¼ c. cornstarch

¼ tsp. salt

3 c. milk (2 percent preferred)

4 egg yolks, lightly beaten

2 Tbsp. butter, softened

1 Tbsp. plus 1 tsp. vanilla

2 large bananas

A heaping teaspoon of playfulness

A sprinkle of mischief

**Putting the Memory Together:**

To make crust, melt butter and add to crackers and sugar. Press into 9"
pie plate and bake at 375 degrees for eight minutes. Meanwhile, stir
together sugar, cornstarch, and salt in saucepan. Blend milk and egg
yolks and gradually stir into sugar mixture. Cook over medium heat,
blending in butter and vanilla. Boil and stir for one minute. Remove
from heat. Press plastic wrap onto surface of filling and cool to room
temperature. Next, peel and slice bananas. Arrange layer of bananas over
cooled pie crust. Pour in cooled filling. Chill for two hours. Decorate

with fresh whipped cream. To be armed and ready for a banana cream pie onslaught, make extra pies and keep them close at hand.

Submitted by: Brooke Palmer, Chicago, IL.

# Top-Secret Cholent

My grandmother, Dinah Pershin, cradled five generations of our family in her arms. She was full of love and showed her affection for her children, grandchildren, great-grandchildren, and great-great-grandchildren with her cooking.

During World War II, her nephew, Warren Shulman, was in the Seabees, stationed overseas. One day, Dinah received a card from Warren, telling her that he was coming to Chicago for a ten day leave and asking that she have some cholent ready and waiting for him. Of course, she was happy to oblige.

A few days after receiving his card, Dinah's doorbell rang. When she answered it, she found two big, burly, serious men standing there. They showed their FBI identification cards and demanded to know what cholent was. While they stood there, very official-like, Dinah explained the entire process of making the special stew. After a detailed description, the men turned away, apparently satisfied. She never heard from them again, and Warren was able to come home for his leave and enjoy his cholent peacefully.

## The Thoughts:

2 pounds short ribs
Shortening
8 potatoes, cut into quarters
6 carrots, cut into large chunks
1 large onion, finely chopped
Salt and pepper to taste
A dash of craving
A dollop of misunderstanding

## Putting the Memory Together:

Brown short ribs in a little shortening. Add onion and sauté slightly. Place half of the potatoes and carrots on the bottom of an ovenproof pot. Add sautéed meat and onions and top with the remaining potatoes and carrots. Season with salt and pepper. Add water to cover. Bring to a boil on the stovetop and then transfer to a 275 degree oven. Bake overnight for about twenty-four hours. Pepper with misunderstanding, garnish with humor, and serve to a favorite relative or any other unexpected guests.

Submitted by Betsy Katz, Highland Park, IL.

# Flamin' BBQ Ribs

My grandpa had many incredible qualities. He was funny, caring, compassionate, wise, kind, and an overall great person. But he was *not* a good cook. So, it's ironic that when I think of him, the first thing that comes to mind is the day I watched him cook ribs. See, my grandparents were always having people over. Whether it was for a holiday, Sunday dinner, or just for fun, they loved to entertain. On this particular Sunday, someone suggested that Grandpa cook ribs instead of ordering them in. This turned out to be a terrible idea.

My grandpa took the ribs out of the oven and asked me to open the sliding glass door that led to the backyard, where he would finish cooking the ribs on the grill. I opened the door and he walked towards the grill, which had been preheating. As he lifted the lid, flames leapt out ferociously. My grandpa closed it quickly to halt their advance.

I couldn't believe what I had just seen. Before even asking if he was okay, I turned to the house to see if anyone else had witnessed what happened. Grandpa seemed oblivious, and he said to me, "Boy, that grill is hot." That's when I noticed that his white-grey eyebrows were *completely* charred. I was speechless. My grandpa had just unknowingly almost lit his entire head on fire, and all he had to say was that the grill was "pretty hot." As we walked back inside to wait for the meat to cook, the first thing my grandma said was, "Howard, what happened to your eyebrows?"

## The Thoughts:

3 racks of baby back ribs
1 bottle Open Pit Original BBQ sauce or sauce of choice
1 tsp. garlic powder
Salt and pepper to taste

## Putting the Memory Together:

Preheat oven to 300 degrees. Place ribs on baking sheet and season on both sides with salt, pepper, and garlic powder. Cover with aluminum foil and cook for two and a half hours. Remove from oven and brush with sauce. Finish cooking ribs on grill over medium (not face-scorching) heat for twenty minutes. Brush with additional sauce as desired. Cut and serve for a sizzling good meal.

Submitted by Ross Samotny, Chicago, IL.

# Perfectly Precise Pecan Sandies

My mother was a fantastic cook. Among the dozens of friends and family she invited over for dinner, there was never anything but praise for her cooking. However, it was an entirely different story when it came to baking. Once, she dove into a new recipe for cookies. Rather than following the recipe explicitly, she concocted the cookies just as she would a pasta recipe or a lamb dish, adding a pinch of this and a dash of that, substituting as she saw fit to accommodate my likes and dislikes. The end result? A batch of pecan sandies *without* the pecans! Needless to say, they did not come out well. I ate the bland, doughy cookies and smiled, trying not to let the disappointment show on my face.

Fast forward to 1995. I was studying abroad in London, and my twenty-first birthday was approaching. My mother always made a big deal about birthdays, and though communication was difficult and I was far from home, she wasn't going to let my twenty-first pass by unceremoniously. I was sitting in my flat when a package arrived. I opened it to find a note that read, "Happy Birthday to my firstborn. Here are your favorite cookies." Inside was a cookie tin chock full of pecan sandies without the pecans. I ate one and told my flatmates they were stale.

These days, I eat pecan sandies with pecans and smile. A baker she was not, but my mom is always in my heart.

## The Thoughts:

½ c. margarine, softened

½ c. vegetable oil

½ c. sugar

½ c. confectioner's sugar, sifted

1 egg

½ tsp. vanilla extract

1 c. all-purpose flour

½ tsp. baking soda

½ tsp. cream of tartar

½ tsp. salt

1 c. chopped pecans (important)

¼ c. white sugar for decoration

A blend of secrecy and humor

A dash of unconditional love

A smile

## Putting the Memory Together:

Put on your birthday hat to make the event a special one, wherever your loved one may be. Preheat oven to 375 degrees. In a large bowl, cream together the margarine, vegetable oil, sugar, and confectioner's sugar until smooth. Beat in the eggs one at a time. Stir in vanilla. In a separate bowl, combine flour, baking soda, cream of tartar, and salt. Stir into the creamed mixture. Fold in pecans. Under no circumstance can you forget the pecans. They are extremely important. Form dough into 1" balls and roll each one in remaining white sugar. Place cookies two inches apart on an ungreased cookie sheet. Bake ten to twelve minutes, or until edges are golden. Cool on wire racks. Send to a loved one far away and know that, good or bad, you'll bring a smile to their face.

Submitted by: Ivy Israel, Chicago, IL.

# Dyer Cream Pie

My father's people were considered "stocky," which was really a euphemism for "small-boned with a lot of extra padding." The source of this chunkiness (something they all had in common) was an insatiable appetite for foods dripping with some form of fat. In my dad's family, a baby was considered flawed unless it was heavily dimpled. So began the child's inexorable path toward stockiness.

My father was probably the most fat-addicted of all of the Dyers. He loved butter so much that he would slap a pat on a bite-sized piece of bread. When he ate popcorn, his real purpose was to get at the butter it was coated in. I'm serious. When he was at home, he would have my mother melt a stick of butter and pour it in a bowl with the popcorn, which he would eat with a spoon—like soup with croutons. While such habits probably did not do much for my dad's arterial health, he did manage to live to the ripe old age of eighty-seven.

With such love for butter, cream, and other rich pleasures, it's only natural that when the Dyer family got together, conversation often turned to delectable dishes. The dish most lauded was Dyer cream pie, a dish that my great-grandmother Dyer had invented. According to family legend, Great-Grandma Dyer used a heavy "farm" cream that could be cut with a knife. When my dad would describe this cream to me, he could hardly contain his longing. There was much competition among the family women (and those brought in by marriage) as to who could bake the finest Dyer cream pie. Some said my Grandmother Dyer was the champ, while others bestowed the title upon one of my aunts. My mother also vied for the top spot, and some relatives said her pie could compete with the best of them. As a result, there was always a Dyer cream pie around to enjoy.

## The Thoughts:

2 c. of the thickest cream you can find (whipping cream works)

1 c. milk

1 c. sugar

3 Tbsp. flour, dissolved in the milk

A pinch of salt

3 egg whites

Pinch of nutmeg

Pie crust (Editor's note: If you'd rather not use a store-bought crust, please see thawed Enid Barnes' "Mom's Perfect Pie Crust")

A heaping tablespoon of longing

## Putting the Memory Together:

Preheat oven to 325 degrees. Combine cream, milk, sugar, flour, and salt. Cook over medium-low heat until thickened. Let cool. Beat egg whites to stiff peaks and then fold into cooled cream mixture. Pour into crust and sprinkle with nutmeg. Bake for forty to forty-five minutes. Watch mouths water. Push aside any guilt and savor each and every bite.

Submitted by Patty Schreiber, St. Charles, IL.

# Mom's Barbecue on a Bun

My parents were Swedish immigrants. With six kids, our house was always bustling and chaotic. We never had a ton of money, but somehow, we always had clothes on our backs and a good meal on the table. While my mom was a sweet, loving mother, my dad was the disciplinarian. When we got in trouble, he was always the one to handle it.

Once, when I was young, my mom made green beans for dinner. I found them gross and didn't want to eat them. I looked around me and noticed this small space between the wall and the refrigerator. It was within arm's reach of my chair at the kitchen table and the perfect size for a thin plate. I figured that as long as my plate was empty, I could be excused. When my parents weren't looking, I grabbed my green beans and tossed them behind the refrigerator. I was so proud—I thought I'd gotten away with it and that I didn't have to eat green beans.

Of course, that night my dad decided to clean behind the refrigerator. (At the time, I couldn't believe it, but now that I'm a parent, I'm sure he had an inkling of what he would find.) I was caught! My dad yelled at me, and from then on, I always ate my green beans.

Here's one of my mom's recipes that I never, ever wanted to throw behind a refrigerator. Enjoy!

**The Thoughts:**

1 lb. ground beef (lean stew beef or roast beef also may be used)
1 onion, chopped
2 Tbsp. dark brown sugar
1 tsp. yellow salad mustard
4 Tbsp. vinegar or sweet pickle juice
1 c. chopped celery
1 c. ketchup
½ c. water
Salt and pepper to taste
Garlic salt or chili powder if desired
A dash of mischief
A sprinkling of humor

**Putting the Memory Together:**

Brown beef lightly and set aside (if using stew or roast beef, slice thinly before cooking). Brown onion in small amount of oil. Add beef and remaining ingredients and simmer for thirty minutes, or until celery is tender. Serve on hamburger buns as a meal or on dinner rolls for an appetizer. So delicious, you'll never have to worry about it being hidden by a finicky young one.

Submitted by Sandy Dickson, Zion, IL.

# Rose's Sneaky Cheese Blintzes

My mother-in-law, Rose, was a riot. She had four sisters who were all very close, and they were great together. They loved to party and laugh and dance, line dancing well into their eighties. They all passed away in their early nineties, including Rose, who passed away when she was ninety-eight and one half years old. She was so disappointed, as she had really wanted to make it to one-hundred years (so she could be on one of those jelly jars).

When I was first married, she said, "There are two things I just can't help you out with: babysitting and cooking." But I later found out that she was holding out on me (at least with the cooking part; she never did babysit.) Since we lived in different states, we visited our in-laws in Florida every Christmas and they stayed with us in Maryland every summer. I did most of the cooking in both places, and my mother-in-law loved it.

One hot, humid summer day when I was extremely pregnant, I felt very crabby and not into cooking at all. So Rose offered to make her cheese blintzes. She spent all afternoon in the kitchen, whipping up these wonderful, light and fluffy blintzes that were cooked to perfection, each one better tasting than the last. I was in heaven! That night, when I set out a bunch for dinner, I also tucked a few dozen way back in the freezer, where nobody else would look. I didn't tell my husband they were there, and for the next month, I would sneak a couple of blintzes each day, savoring them in secret. He never found out, and today, it remains a wonderful, sweet memory!

**The Thoughts:**

Dough:

3 eggs
1 c. milk
2 Tbsp. vegetable oil
½ tsp. salt
¾ c. flour
Butter for frying

Filling:

2 c. farmer cheese
1 egg yolk
2 Tbsp. sugar
½ tsp. vanilla extract
1 Tbsp. butter, melted
A dose of generosity
A spoonful of laughter
A plastic baggie

**Putting the Memory Together:**

Identify a family member or friend who could use a delicious treat. Beat eggs, milk, oil, and salt together in a large bowl. Stir in flour. Heat a small amount of butter in a 6" skillet over medium heat until melted. Pour about 2 Tbsp. of batter into pan, quickly tilting pan until batter evenly coats the bottom. When bottom of blintz is golden brown, carefully turn out onto a paper towel. Continue with remaining batter.

To make filling, mash cheese with fork in a small bowl. Add yolk, sugar, butter, and vanilla. Stir until well blended. In honor of Rose and her sisters, grab a family member and do a little dance.

To assemble, place blintz, brown side up, on a work surface. Spread one heaping teaspoon of filling along one edge of the crepe and roll once to cover filling. Fold the right and left sides over the center and roll, jelly-roll style, until completely closed. Heat a small amount of butter in a skillet over medium heat until melted. Fry blintzes for two minutes on each side. Serve only half of the blintzes with sour cream, if desired. Put the remaining blintzes in a plastic baggie and tuck deep into the freezer, blocking them from view. For the next few days, when no one is looking, sneak a blintz. Savor it, thinking of a loved one.

Submitted by Suzanne Zipkoff, Deerfield, IL.

# Marie's No-Mess Tacos

When I was a kid, we would drive the ten hours from Minneapolis to South Bend, Indiana, to spend at least a week with my grandparents. My grandma, Marie Donchetz, was a great cook, especially when it came to Hungarian dishes. Her parents were from the Old Country, and she would whip up the most delectable chicken paprikash, Szekley goulash, and kolach. Her cupboards were always chock-full of paprika.

But while I liked my grandma's Hungarian cuisine, what I really looked forward to was Taco Night. She would cover her glass kitchen table with bowls of ground beef, taco shells, lettuce, onions, sour cream, and other taco necessities. I would line up with all of my aunts, uncles, and cousins and we'd fill our hard shells and eat our dinner out on the screened in porch, which was my grandma's favorite place in the world. That's when the fun began.

I'd sit across from my grandma and our old competition would begin. I would beg her, "Please, please, please, let's have a contest!" See, on taco night, my grandma and I would always compete to see who could have the fewest pieces of food fall out of their taco shell. Keeping food inside a hard shell is a delicate act, requiring a gentle touch (if you break the shell, you're finished), expert balance (one tip downwards, and you're through) and a supreme focus on the task at hand (turn away for one moment, and anything can happen).

At the end of dinner, we would count how many pieces of tomato, lettuce, beef, cheese, or other crumbs were on our plates. The winner would get an Eskimo Pie and, of course, bragging rights. I would usually win, but I had a secret weapon: during the contest, my grandpa would sit next to me, whispering encouragement in my ear. Sometimes, when my grandma's back was turned, he would grab a tomato or two off of my plate. I would follow his lead, keeping my eyes narrowed in on my grandma the whole time. When my grandpa would declare me victorious, he would wink at my grandma and ask me to grab him an Eskimo Pie, too.

**The Thoughts:**

Hard taco shells
Ground beef
Taco seasoning
Lettuce, chopped
Tomatoes, chopped
Onions, chopped
Salsa
Sour Cream
A competitive edge
A box of Eskimo Pies

**Putting the Memory Together:**

Stock the freezer with Eskimo Pies or other frozen treats. Set the table, alerting fellow family members that a showdown is about to begin. Brown ground beef and lightly season with taco seasoning. Place shells on counter. Scoop tomatoes, lettuce, onions, salsa, and sour cream into serving bowls. Place bowls on counter, near pan of ground beef, and let family members prepare their own tacos. Secure your own designated "secret weapon" and face off. Post victory, be sure to reward him or her with ice cream as well.

Submitted by: Molly Each, Chicago, IL.

# Grandma Angio's Breadsticks

My husband had just picked me up from the airport. I sat in the front seat, my grumbling stomach speaking to the airline's slim pickings on my way back from Florida. When we arrived home, I made a beeline for the refrigerator. As soon as I stepped foot in the kitchen, a familiar smell wafted from the counter: Grandma Angio's breadsticks. My aunt and cousins had just made a fresh batch and dropped them off. I couldn't think of a food that would make me feel more at home. Tears welled up in my eyes as I took my first bite, remembering family gatherings centered around a meal prepared by Grandma Angio.

When we were little, my parents, sister, cousins, aunts, and great-aunts would gather around my grandmother's small kitchen, eager to assist with the meal preparation, under her watchful eye, of course. Little did we know that she had already been cooking all morning and we were merely helping with one small aspect of the meal: her famous breadsticks. As we rolled out the dough, twisting them into not-so-perfect shapes, we would laugh and cry as we told stories (we are Italian after all, passionate about our stories and emotions). Once the breadsticks were pulled out of the oven, we'd move to the plastic-covered couches of my grandma's living room, devouring the breadsticks as a wonderful appetizer. Next, we'd settle in at the dining room table for a huge meal of pasta, pizza, sausages, and meatballs, all made by my grandmother's loving hands.

A few years ago, my sister, our cousins, and I decided we needed to continue our late grandmother's legacy and overcome our fear of failing to live up to her cooking standards. Together as a family, we tried to make her breadsticks. The only problem was that we couldn't decipher what she meant by an "A little of this" and "A little of that." We ruined the first batch and had a pick-up game of hockey with the rock-hard breadsticks. After a few tries, we got it down: "A little of this" is patience, and "A little of that" is, of course, family.

## The Thoughts:

7 c. flour

2 tsp. salt

½ c. Crisco shortening

2 Tbsp. oil

6 eggs

1 c. cold water

½ pkg. dry yeast, dissolved in small amount of warm water

A pinch of home

A heaping spoonful of stories

A sprinkling of humor

## Putting the Memory Together:

First, gather family members together to pool collective recipe knowledge. Working as a team, measure and sift flour and add salt. Work in shortening as though making a pie crust. Make a well in the mixture, and add oil, eggs, water, and dissolved yeast. Dough should be medium consistency. Knead, cover, and let rest. Knead again until smooth. Cover dough and let rest in warm place for one to one and a half hours. Preheat oven to 450 degrees and bring a large pot of water to a boil. Cut dough into small pieces and roll into ropes about 1/2" thick. Drop in boiling water. When breadstick rises to the surface, remove and place on pastry cloth or wax paper. Allow to dry before baking. Bake eighteen to twenty minutes or until brown. Have hockey sticks, baseball bats, and other sporting equipment on hand in case breadsticks come out harder than expected.

Submitted by Alexandra Taylor, Chicago, IL.

# Miss Judy's Jackpot Carrot Cake

My mother never had a sweet tooth. She was a tiny, petite woman who worked out every day and often deprived herself of indulgences. But during the last year of her life, as she battled ovarian cancer, she said, "Screw it!" and finally dug in, enjoying dessert every night. She loved cookies and cakes and anything sweet, but what she really savored was pie. To my delight, once she moved in with my husband and me, I would occasionally wake up in the middle of the night to the scrape of a fork across an empty plate.

Though she spent much of her life avoiding sweets, my mother baked a delicious carrot cake. My husband Bill—her son-in-law, her friend, her caretaker—was a huge fan, and he used to make bets with my mother, always stipulating that if she lost, a carrot cake was to be made. They bet on everything from geography to politics to useless facts, but they most often made bets on grammar. As a teacher, my mom usually won, but whenever she did lose, she baked him her carrot cake. And during the last years of her life, our world was filled with hope, laughter, family, friends, great meals, and, most importantly, sweets.

**The Thoughts:**

Cake:

2 c. sugar

1 ½ c. vegetable oil

3 eggs

2 tsp. vanilla extract

1 tsp. salt

2 ¼ c. flour

2 tsp. baking soda

2 tsp. cinnamon

2 c. shredded carrots

1 8 oz. can of crushed pineapple, drained

1 c. chopped walnuts

2 c. shredded coconut (optional)

A passion for life

A dose of indulgence

A dash of positive thinking

Icing:

8 oz. cream cheese

1 c. powdered sugar

1 tsp. grated lemon zest

As many sweet teeth as you can gather

**Putting the Memory Together:**

First, make a bet with a loved one to see who has to do the baking. The winner sits on the sidelines and scrapes the batter from the bowl while the loser combines sugar, oil, eggs, and vanilla. Sift in flour, baking soda, salt, and cinnamon. Fold in carrots, pineapple, walnuts, and coconut, if desired. Pour into greased and floured cake or bundt pan. Bake at 350 degrees for fifty minutes or until toothpick comes out clean. Meanwhile, make frosting by whipping all ingredients together until smooth. Frost cooled cake. Throw caution—and calorie counting—to the wind and indulge!

Submitted by Erin Passmore, Chicago, IL

# Grandma's Legendary Stuffing

My parents divorced when I was young, so my siblings and I traded off holidays between them. When I was nine years old, we were at my mom's for Thanksgiving. My mom was quite the cook, and every holiday she would wake up at the crack of dawn and never stop moving—chopping, mixing, blending, and setting—until everyone had arrived for dinner. This particular year, I decided I really wanted to help. She put me in charge of the table settings, though I was really eager to be her little sous chef.

By the time I was done with the table, my mom was working on one of my favorite dishes: stuffing. I loved her stuffing—each bite was such a flavor explosion. My mom invited me to help, so I started mixing the breadcrumbs and chopping the celery. My mother turned to me and said, "You know this is your grandmother's recipe, right?" Surprised, I said, "No!"

A wave of sadness rushed over me. Spending holidays with only one of our parents was always a struggle, because it also meant seeing only one set of grandparents. This year, I was missing my father's parents a lot. But my sadness quickly turned to excitement with the knowledge that this was my grandma's recipe. My grandmother rarely cooked (she had very crafty and clever ways of getting out of it!), and when she did, our family usually said that her food was average. But this stuffing was hers—and it was incredible! Mom and I finished cooking the recipe, huge smiles on our faces. Every year after that, my siblings and I laughed as we watched my grandma weasel her out of helping in the kitchen, loving the way we could savor her stuffing without ever watching her make it.

Now, at the age of twenty-six, we have families that separate us and we spend Thanksgiving elsewhere. But I have to smile when I think that one day I'll have a family of my own. I'll host Thanksgiving at my house, make my grandma's stuffing, and laugh when I remember how often she actually made it.

**The Thoughts:**

½ c. butter
1 pkg. herb seasoned stuffing
1 c. finely chopped celery
1 c. chopped white onion, drained well
1 pkg. poultry seasoning mix
¼ c. boiling water
4 c. of gravy-rich chicken stock
1 Tbsp. flour, mixed with drippings from turkey
Pinch of salt, pepper and garlic powder
White wine or sherry to taste
A dash of humor
A sprinkle of surprise

**Putting the Memory Together:**

Find the perfect sous chef. Reveal a family tradition or secret they may not know. Melt butter and pour over stuffing mix. Add veggies and seasonings and toss. Add hot water if needed. Spray casserole dish with non-stick spray. Pour mixture into dish, cover and bake at 350 degrees for forty to forty-five minutes. Serve with gravy. Gather family around and share a favorite, hilarious memory.

Submitted by: Lesley Sarnoff, Chicago, IL.

# Grammie Maggie's "Edges First" Banana Chocolate Chip Cake

Growing up, I was always very close with my grandmother, Dotti. My cousins called her Grammie, and as a young child, I inverted the name and called her Maggie. She liked the name better, so it stuck. Eventually, we all called her Maggie. She loved this banana chocolate chip cake, a recipe that wasn't her own but that she nonetheless demanded at every family gathering.

Maggie always had a strange habit of eating the outsides of bread and baked goods first. It was her favorite part! I have vivid memories of Maggie slicing the banana cake to get the burned edges for herself. My father would slap her hand away for messing up the cake. As the dessert went around the table, Maggie would sneak more and more of the edge until all that was left was a little bit of the center—which, luckily, was my favorite part.

It's been nine years since Maggie passed away, and I have made the cake many times. It doesn't seem to have the same excitement as it did when I would share it with her, but whenever I bake it, I can't help but think that somewhere, she is enjoying it, too.

## The Thoughts:

1 tsp. baking soda
4 Tbsp. sour cream
½ c. butter
1 ¼ c. sugar
2 overripe bananas
2 eggs
1 tsp. vanilla extract
1 ½ c. flour
1 tsp. baking powder
6 oz. chocolate chips
A sprinkle of humor
A dash of joy
Playfulness to taste

## Putting the Memory Together:

Preheat oven to 350 degrees. Put baking soda in a tall glass with sour cream and set aside. Mix together butter, sugar, eggs, bananas, and vanilla. Stir in flour, baking powder, and sour cream mixture. Fold in chocolate chips reserving half a cup to sprinkle on top. Pour mixture in 9" x 9" pan and bake for thirty-five to forty-five minutes. Let cool. Eat the edges first, giving the middle bite to a loved one.

Submitted by: Jennifer Scher, Chicago, IL.

# Opa's Cheesecake

Whenever my grandmother cooked, she used to tease my Opa: "Watch what I'm doing, because I'm going to die someday, and you're going to need to know how to do it." When my grandmother did pass away, suddenly my quiet Opa—who had been the perfect complement to my loud, outspoken grandmother—started to cook. He whipped up delicious soups and gravies, cakes and cookies, entrees and appetizers. We couldn't believe he had been paying attention the whole time!

One of our favorite Opa dishes was his cheesecake. My maternal grandmother was the original source of our family's favorite cheesecake recipe, but Opa made it his own. As soon as the dinner plates were cleared at family parties, we couldn't wait to wolf down a piece of Opa's Cheesecake.

As the years went on, my grandfather became forgetful. He was later diagnosed with Alzheimer's disease, but before that became clear, he would just forget little things. I fondly remember the last time he made his cheesecake masterpiece. My dad, two brothers, and I eagerly cut into the mouthwatering cake, our knives slicing through the sour cream glaze, forks in hand, ready to dive in. We all took a bite and then blinked hard and looked at each other. This was not the cake we had come to know and love! It was slippery, slimy, not at all creamy and completely inedible! My brother asked, "Opa, did you do something different?" We eventually discovered that he had used olive oil instead of butter. We teased him lovingly and today we still crack up every time we talk about it. My grandfather died a few years ago, but we still enjoy his cheesecake. Always remember to use butter!

**The Thoughts:**

Crust:

16 graham crackers, crushed to crumbs
2 Tbsp. sugar
3 Tbsp. melted butter
A pinch of confusion

Filling:

16 oz. cream cheese, softened
1 c. sugar
4 eggs
2 tsp. vanilla
A dash of love

Topping:

½ pint sour cream
2 Tbsp. sugar
1 tsp. vanilla
A heaping spoonful of humor

**Putting the Memory Together:**

Tuck away any bottles of olive oil in the kitchen. Preheat oven to 350 degrees. Mix together crust ingredients and press into bottom of a 9" spring form pan. Bake ten minutes and allow to cool. Beat filling ingredients and pour over cooled crust. Bake forty-five minutes. Remove from oven and increase temperature to 475 degrees. Mix topping ingredients, pour over cake, and bake an additional five minutes. Think of a funny memory and share a laugh together.

Submitted by Angi Holdway, Naperville, IL.

# Chapter 4

## Gratitude through Creativity

**"Gratitude unlocks the fullness of life. It turns what we have into enough, and more. It turns denial into acceptance, chaos to order, confusion to clarity. It can turn a meal into a feast, a house into a home, a stranger into a friend. Gratitude makes sense of our past, brings peace for today, and creates a vision for tomorrow."**

**—Melody Beattie**

Losing a loved one forces you to change your perspective. You look at those around you, helping you through the grief, and hug them a little tighter. You look at your daily routine and realize you need to live more. And as you muddle along, you remember the time you had with your lost loved one and savor every last minute, good and bad. I had my mom for twenty-two years. It's so sad that she's gone, but I'm grateful for every single moment I had with her.

After losing my mom, I discovered exactly how much I knew about cooking—and about hosting elaborate dinner parties. Without my mom and her culinary expertise to lean on, I took on the role of family chef, cooking dinners, whipping up recipes to satisfy my sisters' cravings and hosting holiday celebrations. But I took it to the next level. I challenged myself to cook food that was beyond my mother's repertoire, creating new menus and tabletop settings that ultimately offered a creative outlet for my grief. After losing a loved one, many people sift through their sadness to uncover even a kernel of imagination. It's a welcome distraction, but more than that, it can be a healthy outlet in which to channel your sadness.

"I encourage my clients to find something that might interest them; sometimes painting, sometimes writing, sometimes cooking, something like that," says Jody Schwartz, a Chicago-based psychologist. "Using your hands, your creative side, is attractive to your sensory self and the creative parts of your brain. A sensory part of you might feel comforted, and it might be a thing that brings back memories of places you've been or special foods you like."

For me, cooking was my distraction. My sister Jamie lived in her art, drawing whenever she had a free moment, while my sister Ivy turned to music, attending concerts or holing up in her room with her favorite albums. Though we each chose a different medium (which could be isolating at times), when we came back together, it was as though each of our wounds had healed a bit.

I ask myself often: who would I be if mom had not passed away? That might sound harsh, but when I think about all of the people who have influenced my life—my dad, siblings, friends, extended family, husband, my mother—I have to recognize that I am who I am today because I lost my mom and because I had her.

For some, their life changing event is a major tragedy, like 9/11. For others, it's a fleeting encounter with someone or something that makes them see the world in a different way. But almost everyone can look at their lives and pinpoint the moments when their lives took a significant turn. Some of the things I love most about my life right now—my passion for cooking, my knack for hosting a twenty person dinner party, my commitment to planning charity events for a range of breast cancer organizations (including my mother's foundation)—are a result of losing my mom when I did. That's not to say that I wouldn't trade it all for another moment with my mom. But if I had to lose her, I'm grateful for the course my life has taken since.

Most of all, I've discovered that losing my mom has opened the door to an introspection that I didn't know was there before. It's all part of this chaotic, stuttering way we heal. "The raw feeling we get when we lose a loved one lets us really know we're alive," says Mary Beth Paul, a Chicago-based psychologist. "Give whatever is going on inside you time to surface, and be tuned in to what's happening. It's an opportunity to plumb further into yourself and ask, 'Who is this person?' Or, 'Who am I?'" Paul notes that without that ability to feel, to open up and to truly know ourselves, the loss of a loved will lead to our own emotional death.

It's this opportunity to think and feel differently that has led me to where I am today, and for that I'm most grateful. Before I lost my mom, I never would have dreamed that I would write a book. It's generally hard for me to explain, but after losing my mom, I needed a way to let those emotions out. Being in the kitchen *felt* like the right way, but I didn't know how to pull it all together to make it all complete. When I made "Monday Night Spaghetti" for D.J. one night, happily telling him about our family ritual, it occurred to me that other sufferers probably react to food and cooking in a similar way. Suddenly, this creative side of me came to the surface, and I knew the perfect way to honor my mom.

Putting together this book has been therapeutic for me, and based on the feedback I've received, it has been therapeutic for the participants, too. Flipping through this recipe collection has brought to life memories, images, and details for both the readers and for those who have shared their stories. This has been a healing experience, whether people have been grieving for five months or for fifty years. The opportunity to pour my creative appetite into a project to help others is something that I love and defines my life.

This book is a testament to my mother, my way of giving back to her. I can honor her memory and give meaning to the grief experience. While memories live on in your own heart and mind, putting it down on paper, publishing it and getting it out into the world creates a place in history that no one can take away. This book is something that will help my children learn about their grandma and something for those who are included to pass along to their families. Everyone leaves something on this Earth when they go; perhaps this is mine. Grief is an unavoidable, biological, human emotion, and it can often be a solitary experience. If I've been able to connect anyone to their own process—to their memories or others who may be similarly suffering—I will have honored my mother's memory in the best possible way.

# Mom's Super-Secret Carob Chip Cookies

When I was twelve, I was diagnosed with a heart condition. Known as paroxysmal supraventricular tachycardia, or PSVT, the disorder meant that at any given time, my heart rate could leap from resting to 200 beats per minute. Thus, I was ordered not to have chocolate, caffeine, or stimulants of any kind.

Before I was finally diagnosed, the three years that I spent being poked, prodded, monitored, and tested by dozens of different doctors was a nightmare. Though I dressed like a normal tween, underneath my clothes I was covered in electrode stickers that connected to a heart monitor the size of a pager in a small fanny pack around my waist. On numerous occasions, I would have an episode during class or in the hallway and be rushed to the nurse's office, only to have an ambulance whisk me away to the hospital. It was scary, especially for an almost-teenager who was terrified of being too different.

Though school had become this surreal, uncomfortable experience for me, my mom took the adjustments in stride. Sure, she was there for every appointment, every surgery, every check-up, but her devotion ran much deeper. She bought bigger, baggier sweaters to cover up the heart monitor, and she made a point of treating me like a normal kid around the house. But what I'll always remember is the day I came home from school to find chocolate chip cookies on the table. I had missed sweets so much since my diagnosis, and I was surprised to find them waiting for me.

"Mom, I can't have chocolate!" I protested, upset that I was even faced with such a temptation.

"It's not chocolate," she said playfully, handing me the plate and encouraging me to dig in.

In her effort to ease a difficult situation, my mom had discovered carob chips (which taste almost exactly like chocolate, unless you eat them side by side). I couldn't believe how real they tasted. I ate one cookie, two, then three before my mom could stop me. I had forgotten what I had been missing. After that, my mom went to town with the carob chips, whipping them into cookies, breads, bars, and other sweet treats, always going outside the box and using her creativity to make sure they tasted as normal as possible.

While that time period was the hardest and scariest time of my young life, the tender love and care of my parents always made me feel comfortable, cozy, and accepted, and I am forever grateful for that.

**The Thoughts:**

2 ¼ c. all-purpose four
1 tsp. baking soda
1 tsp. salt
1 c. butter, softened
¾ c. sugar
¾ c. packed brown sugar
1 tsp. vanilla extract
2 large eggs
2 c. carob chips
1 crafty mom

**Putting the Memory Together:**

Preheat oven to 375 degrees. Mix flour, baking soda, and salt in a small bowl and set aside. Beat butter, sugar, brown sugar, and vanilla extract in a large bowl until creamy. Add one egg at a time and beat well. Gradually beat in flour mixture. Fold in carob chips. Drop by rounded teaspoonfuls onto greased baking sheets. Bake for nine minutes or until golden brown. Cool completely and enjoy with the people who accept and love you, imperfections and all!

Submitted by Emily Israel Hoffman, Chicago, IL.

# Mom's Barbecued Spareribs

The following was published in the May 9, 1990, issue of the *Chicago Suburban Times* newspaper. It represents one of my most memorable moments with my mom, who passed away suddenly in June of 1999. She was so happy that Mother's Day. I'll never forget it.

"Happy Mother's Day to all our reader Moms and their families! A special thanks to those who participated in our "Mom's Favorite Recipe" contest. The judges loved Adelaide Pedersen's Barbecued Spareribs recipe, which was submitted by her daughter, Karen Katler. Karen and her mother are from Chicago. Karen wrote: 'At every birthday, we can pick what we want for our birthday dinner, and I always pick Mom's Barbecued Spareribs. They are terrific. For the last twenty years, I've picked Mom's spareribs.' The tasters agreed the ribs were excellent. Cooked to tender doneness, the baby back ribs remained moist and the sauce was rich and mellow with zest, but not too spicy. Karen, her mother, and family will be the guests of The Westin Hotel O'Hare for a deluxe overnight accommodation and Mother's Day brunch in the Astor Ballroom. Mrs. Pedersen's recipe will also be featured on the Bakery Café's daily specials menu during the last two weeks in May."

**The Thoughts:**

3-4 lbs. baby back ribs, cut in pieces
1 lemon
1 large onion
1 c. catsup
⅓ c. Worcestershire sauce
1 tsp. chili powder
1 tsp. salt
2 dashes Tabasco sauce
2 c. water
A tsp. of recognition
A dash of birthday tradition.

**Putting the Memory Together:**

Preheat oven to 450 degrees. Place ribs in shallow roasting pan, meaty side up. Place a slice of unpeeled lemon and a thin slice of onion on each piece. Roast in oven for thirty minutes. Meanwhile, combine remaining ingredients and bring to a boil. Brush ribs with sauce and then lower oven temperature to 350 degrees. Continue baking until tender, about forty-five minutes to one hour. Baste ribs with remaining sauce every fifteen minutes. If it gets too thick, add water. Share the sparerib excitement with those around you, and then celebrate the fabulous meal by treating your family to a deluxe brunch the next day.

Submitted by Karen Katler, Chicago, IL.

# Ruth's Sweet-and-Sour Meatballs

Although my mother, Ruth, was the primary cook in our home, my dad was more than just a guest in her kitchen. He took a starring role after his retirement, when he began to channel his energy into his two favorite hobbies: cooking and vegetable gardening. He learned his skills, no doubt, when he attended Mikvah Israel, the oldest agricultural college in Israel. Mom worked part-time at the Art Institute of Chicago, helping out with special exhibits, and Dad would cook dinner for her. He loved to experiment with things he hadn't cooked before. Mom would ask him to run to the store to pick up something basic—bread or milk—and half the time, he would forget what she sent him for and instead return with an array of exotic ingredients that had caught his eye. My dad also had a terrible sweet tooth and used to hide candy all around the house. After he passed away, my mom found sweets tucked away in the oddest places.

Though my dad's cooking might have been more exotic, my mom's cuisine was still pretty incredible. I've had to approximate most of her dishes, as there are no written recipes—in fact, I can't remember there ever having been a cookbook in our home. She cooked in that intuitive, non-scientific way like cooks of an earlier era. Her sweet-and-sour meatballs are still one of my absolute favorite dishes, and one day before she passed away, I followed her around the kitchen and took notes while she prepared them. They not only taste delicious, but they also smell great while cooking. The aroma is intoxicating, and it never fails to take me back to my childhood and my mom's kitchen.

**The Thoughts:**

1 c. diced carrots
1 c. diced onions
Olive oil
2 cans (14.5 oz.) stewed tomatoes
Salt & pepper
Garlic powder
1 lb. ground beef
1 egg
2 tsp. dried onion flakes
1 onion, grated
½ c. sugar
¼ c. lemon juice
A teaspoon of tradition
A dose of generosity
Culinary adventure to taste
A handful of sweet treats (if you can find them!)

**Putting the Memory Together:**

Bring out the old-fashioned apron. Once you're ready, put away the cookbooks and written recipes. Sauté diced carrots and onions in oil. Add stewed tomatoes (with juice) along with salt, pepper, and garlic powder to taste. Let simmer. To make meatballs, mix ground beef with egg, dried onion flakes, grated onion, and celery. Mix well and season with salt, pepper, and garlic powder. Wet hands and form small meatballs and drop in simmering sauce. Cover and simmer for about thirty minutes. Add sugar and lemon juice. Stir, taste, and adjust the sweet/sour flavor accordingly with additional sugar or lemon juice. Cook for another fifteen to twenty minutes. Have fresh challah on hand for dunking in the sauce! Finish the meal with a sweet treat or a piece of candy, dug out from a loved one's special hiding place.

Submitted by: Belinda Brock, Highland Park, IL.

# Dad's Mountain Artichoke Halibut

My dad was always a mountain man. He had long hair and a beard and loved to work with his hands. In fact, he built almost every house he ever lived in himself. He was friendly and outgoing, but he liked to live surrounded by lots of land, space, and quiet.

As a kid, my family lived in the mountains, out in the boonies. We pretty much lived off of the land. We had a big garden where we grew asparagus, corn, carrots, beets, potatoes, lettuce, squash, and lots and lots of zucchini (my least favorite vegetable, only tolerable when my mom baked it into bread with chocolate). We had goats, and my dad would go out and milk them in the morning. Later, he'd make goat cheese and goat yogurt or trade bottles of milk for eggs from our neighbor down the road.

While my family was very self-sufficient, every now and then my dad would head to town and bring back a treat for my sisters and brothers and I. He would walk through the door with his arms full of artichokes and our mouths would start to water. Maybe it was because they weren't available in our own backyard, but at our house, artichokes were an *event*.

We'd all gather around the table, and Dad would set down a huge plate of steamed artichokes. He'd cover his in mayonnaise, but us kids thought that was gross. We squeezed lemon butter on ours. Then, we would mow them down, dragging the leaves across our teeth to dig out the fleshy part and tossing them carelessly into the middle of the table. I loved being able to eat with my hands, and I loved that artichokes were so messy—from the butter that dripped down my hands to the big pile of discarded leaves on the table.

Now that I'm a chef, I cook a similar kind of rustic-style cuisine. Right now, I'm doing global street food, like Mexican tortas and other handheld eats. I think it's telling that when you ask people what they would want for their last meal, it's often a hamburger, a grilled cheese or something else simple from their childhood. You don't need to give someone a forty-six dollar meal to make them smile.

**The Thoughts:**

10 large (approximately 6 oz. each) fresh Alaskan halibut cheeks
12 baby artichokes
2 fingerling potatoes
2 bunches local greens (chard, spinach, etc.) cleaned, trimmed and chopped
6 lemons
2 c. fresh lemon juice
¼ c. chopped garlic
¼ c. chopped shallots
A small bunch each of fresh parsley, thyme, and oregano
¼ c. grainy mustard
1 c. white wine
½ c. butter
2 c. olive oil
Vegetable oil
Salt and pepper

**Putting the Memory Together:**

Remove all outer dark green leaves of artichokes and place in large pot with two quarts cold water, lemon juice, one cup of olive oil and about four tablespoons of salt. The water should taste slightly acidic and salty. Bring to boil over high heat, then turn down to simmer. Simmer over low heat until cooked through but not mushy, about twenty minutes. You know they're done when a knife slides through effortlessly. Remove from heat, drain most of the liquid, but keep enough to just cover artichokes. Place in ice bath to cool. Once cooled, cut into quarters.

Rinse halibut with cold water and pat dry. Season with salt and pepper. In large sauté pan, heat vegetable oil over high heat until just before smoking. Sear halibut for about one minute, or until it starts to brown, and turn over. Add two tablespoons butter and a few sprigs of each herb. Baste together for one minute. Remove from pan, discard herbs and butter, and keep warm. Trim remaining herbs and chop finely.

In same pan, add half of shallots and garlic and two tablespoons butter. Cook for one minute over high heat. Add wine and juice of four lemons. Reduce until evaporated. Swirl in two tablespoons butter and finish with mustard. Keep warm. In separate pan, add remaining half of garlic and shallots, a pinch of each herb and another two tablespoons of butter. Swirl in pan until soft and aromatic. Add greens and cook, stirring often, until wilted. Add artichokes and a squeeze juice from remaining lemons into pan. Season with salt and pepper.

To plate, place vegetables in center of plate, top with halibut, and drizzle pan sauce around. Enjoy!

Submitted by: Hosea Rosenberg, Boulder, CO
Celebrity Chef

# Mom's Creamy Crunchy Taffy Apple Salad

My mom, Barbara Goldberg, was—and is—the most amazing woman I have ever known. A six year battle with breast cancer cut her life short on July 18, 2006. While she was sick (as on every other day of her life), she maintained a positive attitude that was second to none. She always thought of others first, going above and beyond for her loved ones. Her life was a model of selflessness. She even started an organization at my sister's elementary school called BEAM—But Enough About Me—that encouraged kids to do charitable works.

Nights in our home were quite busy, as my sister and I took ballet classes, and my stepdad owned a shoe store in the suburbs that closed at eight. We would often eat dinner around nine and our likes and dislikes didn't always align. Without complaints, my mom often cooked four separate meals for our family. In one night, she might make bake chicken, boil artichokes, or make pasta and a Caesar salad with homemade dressing. Sometimes we did carry-out, so she would get a break!

The dessert we all loved was taffy apple salad. Making this dish was a two day event, which only built our anticipation. I used to make it with my mom, cutting the apples while she mixed the ingredients. This sweet and crunchy treat has collected many fans over the years. When I took leftovers with me to college, I always returned with requests. Every time I make this salad, it reminds me of the happy times that my mom always brought to others—especially me.

**The Thoughts:**

6 or 7 Granny Smith apples, cubed
1 large can crushed pineapple, drained, juice reserved
1 Tbsp. flour
1 egg
1 ½ Tbsp. white vinegar
1 c. sugar
2 c. mini marshmallows
1 ½ c. chopped cocktail peanuts
8 oz. Cool Whip
A dollop of selflessness
A teaspoon of generosity

**Putting the Memory Together:**

Round up your favorite kitchen assistant to help cut you the apples. In saucepan, combine pineapple juice, flour, egg, vinegar, and sugar. Stir and cook until thick. Refrigerate overnight. The next day, mix in apples, marshmallows, pineapple, and peanuts. Top with Cool Whip and enjoy!

Submitted by Jessica Raskin, Chicago, IL.

# Mom's Homemade Red Velvet Cake

I've worked at a newspaper—the *Daytona Beach News-Journal*—for many years. My mom, Mary Carter, used to run the cafeteria, and everyone loved her. Every day the entire menu was homemade, and the staff used to hurry to the cafeteria to devour delicious offerings like Italian chicken. She was one of nine kids and grew up during the Depression: she could take a little bit of nothing and make a special meal.

The two of us were recipe scavengers. Once we saw a new dish in a book or magazine, we rushed out to get the ingredients to make it. We found the recipe for red velvet cake in a newspaper, and Mom quickly added it to the cafeteria's lineup. It was the biggest hit with rich cake layers soaked in hot, sweetened milk—plus there was the Southern allure of the dish. The results were out of sight. The red velvet cake became a best seller. She would often make it on request for employee birthdays and even on the side for folks who asked.

After retiring, she continued to bake the cakes for fans of the deep red confection. I'm still at the newspaper, but the cafeteria no longer serves up homemade food. Rather, it's lined with vending machines. It makes me sad to go up there and remember my mom behind the counter, bringing so much joy to everyone every single day.

It's been four years since she passed, and I miss her terribly. At her memorial service, I spoke of my love and respect for her and of how much she had taught me—especially cooking. I made a few red velvet cakes for the reception after the service, because when I put that big mixer on the counter and assemble the ingredients for a cake, I know she's there with me.

**The Thoughts:**

Cake:

2 c. all-purpose flour
1 tsp. baking powder
1 tsp. salt
1 tsp. cocoa
¾ c. vegetable oil
1 ½ c. sugar
2 eggs
1 oz. bottle of red food coloring
1 c. buttermilk
1 tsp. baking soda
1 tsp. vanilla
A spoonful of cheer

Glaze:

¾ c. milk
½ c. sugar

Frosting:

8 oz. cream cheese, softened
¼ c. butter
1 tsp. vanilla extract
½ c. Confectioner's sugar

**Putting the Memory Together:**

Preheat oven to 350 degrees. For cake, sift together flour, baking powder, salt, and cocoa into a bowl and set aside. Cream oil and sugar. Add eggs one at a time, beating well after each addition. Add food coloring, mixing well at slow speed until blended. Combine buttermilk with baking soda and mix well. Add to oil-sugar mixture, alternating with dry ingredients. Add vanilla and mix well. Spoon into two prepared 9" round cake pans. Bake twenty-five to thirty minutes. Cool in pan for ten minutes, remove and place on a baking rack. Place racks over dinner plate or tray to catch drips from glaze. To make glaze, combine milk and sugar in a sauce pan. Bring to a boil, stirring constantly. Spoon mixture evenly onto each layer before frosting. To make frosting, blend cream cheese and butter until smooth. Add confectioner's sugar and vanilla and mix well. Frost cake. Serve to those who may need a midday boost. Keep refrigerated after serving. Take requests for the next batch, baking them up with a giant helping of love.

Submitted by Kathy Kelly, Daytona Beach, FL.

# Esther's "Everything Fried is Better" Kreplach

My husband's grandmother, Esther, was simply one of those women everyone loves. Her greatest pleasure in life was seeing her family gathered around her table every Friday night. While we looked forward to any meal at her house, we couldn't wait for Rosh Hashanah, when she would serve a more than ample supply of kreplach. These were no ordinary kreplach. As a special treat for her family, she would fry them because, as her son, Allen, would say, "Everything fried is better!"

Back in the 1960s and 70s, armed with a small kitchen, no food processor and one frying pan, she would single-handedly make several hundred kreplach for our family on her own. One year, I was lucky enough to have her prepare them in my kitchen, where she shared the secrets to her recipe. Since her death, her legacy has endured, as we gather at my home each year to make kreplach. Today, the process has evolved from a one woman show into a family event.

The night before kreplachfest, I prepare the meat mixture (multiplying the below recipe by five). Early the next morning, Uncle Allen and cousin Chick arrive with their pasta-making machine. I prepare the dough, and they run it through the machine, laying the rows of dough on my kitchen table to "breathe" until we're ready to fill them.

Throughout the day, dozens of relatives stop in for an hour or so to help Jenny and Stephanie fill the dough. At times, we've had ten people in the kitchen at once, taking turns filling. Next, the kreplach is boiled in water, supervised by Aunt Kaye. The final stage is the frying, which we've moved outside to take advantage of our turkey fryer. This is my husband Michael's domain. By the end of the day, thanks to an enthusiastic family and our on-point assembly line, we'll have made 400.

Every year we laugh that Grandma Esther is looking down, amazed that the simple one-woman process she used to know now takes so many people and so much equipment.

**The Thoughts:**

Filling:

2 lb. chuck steak
1 lb. sliced onions
½ lb. chicken liver
3 chopped garlic cloves
3 eggs
Salt and pepper to taste
A sprinkle of teamwork
A heaping spoonful of anticipation and excitement

Dough:

1 ¾ c. lukewarm water
4 c. flour
4 eggs, beaten
Oil for frying
Humor to taste

**Putting the Memory Together:**

Meat Filling:

Assemble a crew of kreplach-loving family members. Assign roles in the assembly line. Preheat oven to 350 degrees. Sauté meat, onions, chicken livers, and garlic together for two and a half hours, or until tender. Chop in food processor and combine with eggs, salt, and pepper.

Dough:

Blend water, flour, and eggs, adding flour gradually until dough is slightly stiff. Roll out dough and cut into small 3" squares. Add a teaspoon of meat filling to the middle of each square and fold into triangle, twisting ends together. Cook in boiling water for three to five minutes, then fry in oil. Before digging in, stop and take in the incredible amount of kreplach, savoring the sight of what a family can do together.

(Note: We typically prepare them a couple of weeks before the holidays, freeze and take out when needed, reheating them in the oven.)

Submitted by Debbie Lorsch, Buffalo Grove, IL.

# Sandrik-Luedtke-Paulus Plum Dumplings

My grandparents came to the United States from Czechoslovakia, bringing with them family recipes passed down for generations. We would visit them on weekends. My grandmother, Victoria, a short, round woman who loved to talk about the old country, was an early riser. When I opened my eyes in the morning, the house would already be filled with the aroma of food she had been preparing for hours. I would join her and watch her cook, admiring how she stretched dough for apple strudel or boiled berries for jam. It was so different from the way my mom cooked.

My grandparents had a small cottage on Moccasin Lake, and when we would stay with them, I could see the true breadth of my grandma's cooking abilities. After chores, she would hand me a coffee can that I would fill with freshly picked raspberries, blueberries, and blackberries for us to make into jam. When I was up extra early, I would head outside to the lake with my grandparents to catch fish for breakfast. We ate whatever we could get.

I finally began to learn my grandma's recipes through trial and error, as all of her recipes were written in Czech (except for the measurements). After she passed away, I asked my mother, who had never made my grandma's plum dumplings, to try it with me. It took a few rounds, but eventually, we had plum dumplings that were just like Grandma's. I remember thinking how proud she would have been. Every summer, when the plums are in season, my mom and I make batches for our entire family. Though people are unsure at first, they eventually come to love them. I've passed the recipe on to many to keep the memories of my Grandma Sandrik and my mother, Gert Luedtke, alive.

**The Thoughts:**

4 potatoes, boiled and mashed
1 Tbsp. butter
1 egg + 1 yolk
1 ½ c. flour
½ teaspoon salt
12-20 Italian prune plums (found in late summer only)
A heaping spoonful of patience (during fall, winter, spring, and early summer)
A sprinkle of surprise
A dash of tradition

Topping:

½ c. butter
2 c. plain bread crumbs
1 tsp. cinnamon
½ c. sugar

**Putting the Memory Together:**

Mix potatoes with butter and set aside to cool. Add eggs, flour, and salt to form a dough. Knead dough by hand for ten to fifteen minutes. Flour a board and roll out to quarter inch thickness. Using a sharp knife, cut dough into squares large enough to cover plums. Wrap dough around plum, making sure no holes form. Set aside on floured surface. Meanwhile, make topping by melting butter in a frying pan and adding plain bread crumbs, cinnamon, and sugar. Fry on low heat, stirring often, until crumbs are brown. Bring a large pot of water to a boil and carefully drop in wrapped plums. Let dumplings rise to the top and then cook three to five minutes longer. Remove with slotted spoon and roll in topping. Serve warm, cut open, and sprinkled with sugar. Pass along to family and friends, accompanied by a written recipe.

Submitted by: Karen Paulus, Brown Deer, WI.

# Greg's Award-Winning Barbeque Rub

A U.S. Navy Officer and engineer by trade, my husband, Greg, knew his way around the kitchen. His father liked to cook, and when my husband was as young as nine, he was experimenting in the kitchen, whipping up lemon meringue pies for his parents and brothers. Throughout his life, he always strove to be the best at everything he did, and cooking was no exception. He studied cooking like a science, taking notes as he watched cooking shows on television and reading books to refine his already amazing skills. He always seized the opportunity to learn. He took a cooking class on a vacation to Thailand and a barbecue class taught by a Kansas City master when we lived in Louisiana during which he earned first prize and a blue ribbon for his BBQ rub. He loved to try out new creations and was always improving on his latest success. Lucky for me (and our two loyal dogs), we got to indulge in the goodness of his efforts each day.

Being the fun-loving guy that Greg was, he loved to entertain. He thoroughly enjoyed bringing family and friends together, watching the joy he could deliver through food. He became the neighbor that you hoped would invite you over for a Sunday of NFL football, just so you could enjoy the smoked brisket that he'd been preparing all morning. Greg was a fabulous host throughout the year, but his favorite family gathering was Thanksgiving. He went all out—even the two years when it was just the two of us—researching and preparing the most gourmet version of every traditional dish and serving them up with perfect presentation. Not a day goes by that I don't miss Greg's cooking, and the sentiment is echoed often by family and friends, who call to ask for some of their favorite Greg recipes. We can all only hope that our creations measure up to Greg's!

## The Thoughts:

¼ c. sugar

¼ c. garlic salt

¼ c. jalapeno salt

¼ c. onion salt

¼ c. dark chili powder

¼ c. black pepper

¼ c. paprika

¼ c. granulated garlic

¼ c. white pepper

1 tsp. cayenne pepper

1 Tbsp. cumin

1 Tbsp. orange peel

A dash of learning

A heaping spoonful of creativity

## Putting the Memory Together:

Mix all ingredients together. Apply by rubbing onto meat, coating all surfaces with a thin layer. If rub isn't sticking well, apply a thin layer of olive oil. Store remaining rub in an airtight container. It's delicious on any meat or poultry and is especially tasty on a smoked Thanksgiving turkey. Try it out, evaluate, and improve.

Submitted by: Kristin Gebbie, Charleston, SC.

# Giuseppe's Sunday Morning Frittata

Every Sunday morning, my husband, Giuseppe Pecoraro, would get up at dawn, brew a pot of coffee, and head to the local farmers market. He would arrive there as early as 6 a.m., which he insisted was the best time to scoop up the "good stuff." He'd come home, whip up a frittata, and bring it to me while I was still in bed. He never followed recipes: he was all about flavors. I'd wake lazily to Giuseppe coming through the bedroom door carrying a tray decked out not only with the frittata but also with flowers, Italian pastries, and a trinket or two he had found at the market.

We were married for just two years before he died. In that short time, he taught me to be more patient and giving, to not take life so seriously, and to live each day like it was my last. After he passed away, I quit my fast paced job in the fashion industry, realizing I wasn't the same person that I was when we had met. He used to say that every day, you should be kind to someone, make someone laugh, and be creative. His accent and cooking (especially that frittata) swept me off my feet, but it was his perspective on life that made me fall head over heels in love.

**The Thoughts:**

12 large potatoes

1 c. Parmesan cheese

2 c. bread crumbs

2 large eggs, beaten

1 medium yellow onion

1 loaf Italian bread

A sprinkling of gratitude

A heaping cupful of romance

A bouquet of flowers

**Putting the Memory Together:**

As the sun rises, start up a pot of coffee for any loved ones and head out to the farmer's market for the best possible produce. Return home quickly. While family is still sleeping, peel potatoes and shred with a grater. Rinse in cold water. Remove excess water, pat dry, and put in large mixing bowl. Shred onion, squeeze out excess liquid, and add to potatoes. Mix in eggs and Parmesan cheese and mix well.

Add cooking oil into large frying pan over medium heat. Pour in egg mixture and brown on both sides. When finished, set on a paper towel. Place inside sliced Italian bread, like a sandwich. Pile onto a tray and serve to unsuspecting (or secretly suspecting) loved ones. After breakfast, conquer the world and live life to the fullest.

Submitted by: Gladys Najar, Bolingbrook, IL.

# "Mom's so Proud" Birthday Banana Bread

My mom, Suzanne, loved to cook. She found such solace in the kitchen, maneuvering around our wraparound kitchen island and humming to herself or listening to music. She watched the Food Network, subscribed to cooking magazines and went all out for holidays and festive gatherings. She always urged my sister and me to branch out and try new foods, but we were always content with the simple fare: meatloaf, casseroles, and grilled cheese. My mom truly flourished as a cook once we left home—probably because she wasn't limited to kid-friendly recipes anymore.

Not surprisingly, it was my mom's goal in life to get my sister and me cooking. She would buy us cookbooks, peddle subscriptions to *Bon Appetit,* and email us recipes, saying, "You should try this; it's really easy to make!" One Christmas, she even bought me a new set of pots and pans—even though a hectic work schedule had me eating bowls of cereal and frozen dinners every night. When I would actually try something out (usually a simple project like brownie mix), she'd joke, "I can't believe you turned on the oven."

My mom felt such joy when cooking or baking. You could always see the pride in her smile when, of course, her dish was a hit. I was proud of her, and every time, I would resolve that this year I would start cooking. Since her passing, I haven't let my crazy work schedule get in the way anymore. Once a week, I make it a point to cook something from scratch. When I have friends over for dinner, I pull recipes off of her favorite websites. For all of the intricate and complex recipes she tried and perfected, my very favorite is still my mom's banana bread, which was a staple on my birthdays when I was young. Isn't it the little things we always miss the most?

## The Thoughts:

2 large eggs

¾ c. sugar

1 c. smashed very ripe bananas (about 3 medium)

⅓ c. buttermilk

1 Tbsp. vegetable oil

1 Tbsp. vanilla extract

1 ¾ c. all-purpose flour

2 tsp. baking powder

½ tsp. baking soda

½ tsp. salt

A pinch of joy

A dash of promise

## Putting the Memory Together:

Start with a dusting of well-intentioned parental pressure, than eliminate any palate timidity. Next, preheat oven to 325 degrees. Lightly grease 8 ½" x 4 ½" x 2 ½" pan and dust with flour. Beat eggs and sugar in large bowl with electric mixer until thick and light, about five minutes. Mix in smashed bananas, buttermilk, oil, and vanilla. Sift flour, baking powder, baking soda, and salt into mixture and beat until just blended. Transfer batter into pan. Bake until bread is golden brown on top, about one hour. Cool on rack. Savor the aroma of perspective. You can lightly toast the slices when ready to eat. And don't forget the candles.

Submitted by: Katherine Jones, Columbus, OH.

# Grandma Myrt's Farmhouse Potato Salad

When I think of my grandma, Myrtle Fay, I remember her hands most clearly. Delicate yet sturdy, they perfectly suited her life as the wife of a farmer. In the summers, our large family would gather at my grandparents' house in the country. The boys would work in the yard and garden with my grandfather while the women would work feverishly in the kitchen with Grandma Myrt putting together lunch. Even when we were serving simple ham or turkey sandwiches, Grandma Myrt would always serve her signature potato salad on the side. I can still see her delicate hands decked with antique rings and slicing the warm potatoes right in the palm of her hand with a wooden handled antique knife.

As a tribute to my Grandma Myrt, we now regularly make her signature potato salad in our family catering business. It's a favorite among our customers, who are certain we have a secret ingredient that makes the salad so irresistible. But I think the difference is in Grandma Myrt's technique: slicing the potatoes right in your palm, while they're still warm. Even now, taking a bite brings me back to those warm summer days at the farmhouse. Still, without the loving care of Grandma Myrt's hands, it's never quite the same.

**The Thoughts:**

10 lbs. red, waxy potatoes, scrubbed clean
8 eggs, hard-boiled and chopped
6 stalks celery, chopped
1 yellow onion, diced
Kosher salt
Fresh ground pepper
A pinch of legacy

Dressing:

4 c. mayonnaise
1 Tbsp. celery seeds
1 Tbsp. yellow mustard
3-4 tsp. pickle juice

**Putting the Memory Together:**

Before beginning, notice the hands of your fellow chefs, taking in their nooks, crannies, and characteristics. Embed it in your memory. Next, load potatoes into a tall stockpot and cover with water. Cook over medium-high heat for twenty-five to thirty minutes, monitoring carefully when potatoes come to a boil, so as to not overcook. They're done when a knife goes through easily. Remove from heat and drain. Let potatoes cool until they can be comfortably handled. Meanwhile, layer eggs, onion, and celery in a large mixing bowl. Salt and pepper each layer to taste. Peel still-warm potatoes with a paring knife. Dice carefully in the palm of your hand and add to mixing bowl. Season to taste and mix lightly. To make dressing, whisk together all ingredients. Add to salad in small batches, tossing gently each time, until desired consistency is reached. Refrigerate any remaining dressing, which can be added to leftovers if salad becomes dry. Serve to family, friends, and strangers, carrying on a family legacy through food.

Submitted by: Emily Cotton, Peoria, IL.

# Jene's Generous Goulash

My mother, Christina, met my father, Jacob, on New Year's Day, 1900. They met through my mother's cousin, and my mother would later say, "He took a shine to me." After serving in the Spanish-American War, my father had worked as a grocer, then as a butcher. His store was full of chopping blocks and sparkling clean glass cases filled with chops and steaks, and the floor was always covered in sawdust. In the spring, he would always adorn the cases with pails filled with beautiful, fragrant lilacs. Jacob loved his customers, and if he heard there was an illness in their families, he would ask Jene (his loving nickname for my mother) to make a pot of goulash for the family.

Indeed, my father always helped out. Occasionally, people would walk into his butcher shop and ask for some extra bones for their dogs. But my father knew the bones were really for the customer's family. He would always leave a little extra meat on the bones to help them out. Even the nuns would come in, hearing of his generosity, to ask for meat to take back to the convent for the hungry. I didn't appreciate it then, but now I see how much good he did for those in need. Now, when I make his goulash, I cherish and honor his truly giving spirit.

**The Thoughts:**

1 lb. lean ground beef

6 oz. can tomato paste or canned tomatoes

2 medium onions, diced

1 medium carrot, diced

½ tsp. caraway seeds

Rice or noodles, for serving

Bread crumbs, for serving

Several tablespoons of generosity

**Putting the Memory Together:**

Brown the beef in a frying pan, then add tomato paste or canned tomatoes. Salt and pepper to taste. Add onions, carrot, and caraway seeds. Simmer until meat and vegetables are tender. Serve with boiled rice or noodles, garnished with browned breadcrumbs and a vase of lilacs on the table. Always make a bit extra for any friends or loved ones who may stop by.

Submitted by Helen Ruth McCann, Jersey City, NJ.

# Mom's Old-Fashioned Custard Ice Cream

I grew up during the Depression in South Bend, Indiana. I had five brothers and sisters, and my dad was often out of work. We didn't have a lot of money, but my family had a community garden, and every Sunday, my parents' friends would help with the planting, weeding, and sowing. After the women prepared a potluck lunch, my mom would use rich goat's milk to make vanilla ice cream by hand. She would put the mixture into one of those hand-crank ice cream makers and, after the men churned it, the mixture went into our big ice cream freezer.

While the ice cream froze, we would all go back to the garden. But this time, we played. We ran around, played games, and went swimming. When we were tuckered out, we would head back inside and savor every last bite of vanilla ice cream. It was my favorite dessert as a kid, and when I eat it now, it reminds me of my childhood.

**The Thoughts:**

A cupful of history

2 c. milk

1 c. sugar

6 egg yolks, beaten

2 Tbsp. vanilla extract

4 c. whipping cream, chilled

A dollop of teamwork

A teaspoon of community

**Putting the Memory Together:**

Pour milk into double boiler over medium heat. Bring the milk to a gentle simmer and then remove from heat. In a separate bowl, combine the sugar, salt, and yolks. Whisk or beat with hand mixer until mixture has thickened enough to hold a trailing pattern on the surface for two or three seconds, or about three minutes. Gradually add the scalded milk to the egg mixture. Beat or whisk while slowly pouring in a cup of milk at a time. Do not overbeat; mix just until combined. Once all the milk has been added, pour back into double boiler. Cook custard over medium-low heat until almost boiling and thick enough to coat the back of a spoon. Stir constantly, scraping sides, and bottom of pan. Do not allow the custard to boil, or it may curdle. If it does curdle, pour through a strainer. Remove custard from heat and allow to cool. Pour into a glass bowl and cover the surface with plastic wrap to prevent a film from forming. Refrigerate for at least four hours, preferably twenty-four. Stir in cream and vanilla and mix well. Process in ice cream maker according to manufacturer's directions. Best served with a group of family, friends, and community

Submitted by Virginia Working, South Bend, IN.

# Making the Best out of Bruised Potatoes

My nana, Rosie, lost her mom when she was eleven years old. It was the early 1920's and Rosie became solely responsible for her six siblings while her father worked as hard as he could to provide for the family. She cooked, cleaned, laundered, and abandoned all hope of ever having a childhood of her own.

Five long, hard years later, along came a handsome twenty-six year old man from Italy named Mike. He was smitten with Rosie from the minute he laid eyes on her, and soon after meeting, he asked for her hand in marriage. She agreed under one condition: that he would allow her four youngest siblings to move in with them. Without hesitation, he said yes.

Rosie was married at sixteen, had her first baby at eighteen, and settled happily into their life as her siblings left the nest, one by one. Their home was full of joy, the family always cooking, singing Italian songs, drinking homemade wine, and dancing. The hardship of those first five motherless years was but a distant memory. Now, Rosie had a beautiful, loving family.

It was the love, energy, and passion she had for her family that Nana and I talked about when we baked and cooked together. She was a cook, not a chef. When I would take her to the grocery store, she would always buy the bruised and reduced produce. It was part of her history: her special talent for turning something seemingly bad into something indescribably delicious. There wasn't a vegetable she couldn't conquer or an ingredient that wouldn't make you beg for more. Often I would ask for the recipe for these famous dishes, but no such thing existed. She would just laugh and say, "Just watch me."

I did. Now, I, too, am a cook. I can throw together just about any vegetable dish with relative success. These days, I feel her presence as I slice my ingredients or reach for my olive oil and crushed red pepper.

**The Thoughts:**

2 Tbsp. olive oil
2 red potatoes, peeled and thinly sliced
3 eggs
1 green pepper, diced

**Putting the Memory Together:**

Heat oil in a medium pan. Add potatoes and cook until golden brown. Add green pepper and cook until tender. Whisk eggs together and pour over potato mixture. Cook until eggs are set. Marvel at the beauty of making something from almost nothing and enjoy.

Submitted by Evie Thies, Orland Park, IL.

## Mom's Summer Pineapple Cherry Treat

In the kitchen, my mom was an eye-baller. She could take three random ingredients from a seemingly empty refrigerator and turn them into a tasty dish or find a couple leftover tidbits in our cupboards and transform them into a great dinner. Nothing had a recipe. In the rare case that it did, it was written in her native Macedonian, which I didn't understand, or in unintelligible English which I also didn't understand on disorganized pieces of scrap paper. I never tried to cook with her or watch her work in the kitchen, and after I lost her to a long battle with breast cancer, one of the first things that crossed my mind was, "Oh, no! I never learned how to cook from my mom!"

For several years, I was frustrated, but after I graduated from college and started cooking regularly, I discovered that I, too, am an eye-baller. I realized that I didn't need recipes to figure out some of my mom's best dishes. She passed down to me the ability to turn a couple of ingredients into something special, like this refreshing dessert, which I whipped up with a bag of walnuts (a staple in my house growing up). Now, my boyfriend calls me "MacGyver in the kitchen." I know that would make my mom proud.

**The Thoughts:**

1 can (21 oz.) cherry pie filling
2 c. fresh pineapple (or 20 oz. drained, crushed pineapple)
1 c. chopped walnuts
8 oz. Cool Whip
¼ c. sweetened dried coconut (optional)

Combine all ingredients in a bowl and mix thoroughly, until the mixture is evenly pink in color. Top with coconut if desired. Chill and serve cold. Tastes great served with graham crackers and a crafty cooking attitude.

Submitted by: Yasemin Zeytinoglu, Chicago, IL.

# About the Author

Growing up, Emily Israel Hoffman spent many apron-clad hours in the kitchen alongside her mother, Renée Israel. Days were spent prepping, making grocery lists, and heading to market. Nights were spent cooking and enjoying delectable dishes with family. Every Sunday night, the Israel household became the culinary epicenter of their North Shore Chicago neighborhood as dozens of friends and extended family members gathered to enjoy Renée's gourmet cuisine and expertly executed hostess skills. After constant compliments to the chef, Renée and her friends published two cookbooks entitled *Whip Me, Beat Me, Eat Me—Making Memories.*

As her mother saw success with her cookbooks, Emily paved her own way. After graduating from Lake Forest College with a Bachelor's Degree in Communications, she worked in sales and real estate but never lost sight of her love of cooking. In October 2001, Emily's mother was diagnosed with breast cancer. After a battle fought with dignity and grace, Renée passed away on January 23, 2006. Reeling from the profound loss, the Israel family started the Renée Israel Foundation, which benefits breast cancer research. Through this organization, the family created a third edition of *Whip Me, Beat Me, Eat Me* in memoriam of Renée.

Though these bittersweet pursuits filled Emily with a temporary sense of purpose, they did not offer the total solace that she sought as she struggled with the grief of losing a loved one. One day, craving the comfort of her mother's kugel, Emily pulled out her mother's recipe and began to cook. She found that felt more connected to her mother than ever before. Cooking became therapeutic, a method of coping with her grief and a way to feel close to her mother. With the support of friends and family, Emily whipped up *A Blending of Bittersweet Memories*, a cookbook dedicated to those who have lost a loved one. The compilation of endearing stories and family recipes—

gathered from people all over the world—will allow their legacies and bittersweet memories to live on forever.

This book was compiled, written, and edited with the help of Molly Each, a Chicago based freelance writer. Specializing primarily in style, travel, and food writing, her work has been featured in the *Chicago Tribune*, the *Tribune Magazine*, *CS*, *Time Out Chicago*, *Where Chicago*, espn.com, playboy.com and on Chicago Public Radio. Her nonfiction essays have been published on Toasted-Cheese.com and FreshYarn.com and in a variety of literary magazines, including *Annalemma Quarterly* and *Hair Trigger*. She has twice been a Ragdale resident and is currently working on several nonfiction projects.

# Acknowledgements

*A Blending of Bittersweet Memories* could never have happened without the love, devotion, support, and expertise of an amazing collection of people. I am overwhelmed with gratitude for the efforts of many, including:

My friend Jennifer Scher, who, over dinner, pushed me to pursue this small idea. The result has been a project that has helped me grieve, find my passion, and do something to help others. From her initial nudge, I followed a dream.

My friend Dana Levy, who guided me into the right direction with all of her amazing contacts.

Zapwater PR, who helped me get the publicity I needed (via television, magazines, newspapers, and blogs) to attract the number of submissions needed to create a great book.

The psychiatrists and psychologists who took the time to offer their insight and expertise.

Lisa Mollo of Digit-L Web Services, who created and maintained my website along with designing the book cover.

Adam Kaplan of Senior Lifestyle Corporation and Cade Mlodinoff at Barton Senior Residences of Zion, who allowed me to put on cooking demonstrations, talk to, and interview their senior residents, chock full of amazing stories.

My editor, Amy Hall. Thank you for taking the time to edit and proofread the book. You were the last piece of the puzzle, and I can't thank you enough for your hard work.

Everyone who submitted a recipe. Whether it was included in the final collection or not, thank you for sharing a piece of your life with me. I've enjoyed reading your stories and trying your recipes, and I appreciate your generosity in sharing something so intimate with the world.

My sisters, in-laws, aunts, uncles, cousins, and friends, who supported me throughout the project. Thank you for always keeping our family tightly knit, for always being close, for dining around the table, and for never forgetting our holiday traditions or Sunday night dinners. I will do my very best to continue all of it.

Molly Each, my co-writer. She sorted through all of my ideas, excitement, and disorganized thoughts to help turn chaos into something honed, organized, and tasty. Thank you for the endless hours you spent contacting submitters, listening to their stories, and forming them into what they are today. Your creativity and support have turned a small idea into a book.

My dad. Through it all, no matter how bad things were, he always saw the best in me, even when I felt like an outcast. His number one concern is my happiness, and he always supports me in every adventure. He was a wonderful husband to my mom, and the two of them gave me the most beautiful example of a relationship, one that I strive to live up to on a daily basis.

And to you, my husband, D.J. When we first met, life was simpler. All we had to worry about was getting dressed to the nines and having a blast. However, it wasn't until life became more difficult for me that I uncovered the true warmth of your heart and the true depths of your soul. During my darkest hours, when my mother was growing weaker until she passed away, you stood by me. Even when I tried to push you away, you wouldn't leave my side. We were young, and you deserved to live life to the fullest—not to be constrained by my hurdles, particularly during the grieving process I was about to struggle through. I know my mother is watching over me, because I am truly blessed to call myself your wife. You have encouraged me every step of the way as I embarked on the journey to healing and as I brought this book to fruition. When I needed you, you never grew impatient with me. You put aside your doubts and tasted every single recipe. I look forward to a lifetime of our own Sunday night dinners with the family we have and will continue to grow.

I love you.